The Real
Joyce Compton

Also by Michael G. Ankerich

Broken Silence: Conversations with 23 Silent Film Stars (McFarland & Co., 1993)

The Sound of Silence: Conversations with 16 Film and Stage Personalities Who Bridged the Gap Between Silents and Talkies (McFarland & Co., 1998)

**BEHIND THE
DUMB BLONDE
MOVIE IMAGE**

The Real
Joyce Compton

**BY JOYCE COMPTON
AND MICHAEL G. ANKERICH**

Published in the USA by:
BearManor Media
P O Box 71426
Albany, Georgia 31708
www.bearmanormedia.com

ISBN 1-59393-457-2

Printed in the United States of America.
Book design by Brian Pearce.

TABLE OF CONTENTS

Acknowledgements 9

Biography and Interview. 11

A Note on the Memoir 37

My Beginnings 45

A Death in the Family 53

Discovering the Facts of Life and Other Teenage Difficulties 57

Hollywood, Here I Come!. 63

My Break into the Movies 69

I Become a Baby Again, a Wampas Baby 79

An Education in Studio Politics 83

A Romance at First National. 87

The Freedom of Freelancing 91

Clara and I Break into the Talkies 95

Salute! 101

Joycie, Janet, and Joel at Fox. 107

Living the Hollywood Life. 115

We Lose it All. 125

Out Foxed 129

New York, New York 135

Dear Abby 139

Back to Work 145

House Plans and a Final Abby Episode 153

How to Build a House from Scratch 157

Rustling with the Cowboys 161

The Lear Jet Set and Other Hollywood Adventures 167

Cary Grant and "The Awful Truth" 173

The Glamorous and Bejeweled Chickie 177

The Fur Flies 181

I Keep my Bangs 187

"A Southern Yankee" and Some of the Men in my Life .191

Forming the Hollywood Christian Group 201

I Become a Prisoner 205

Losing my Rock of Gibraltar 209

My Attempt at Every Day Work 213

My Fling with a Gay Minister 217

I Tie the Knot, or Does it Tie Me? 223

Finding my way after Bill 235

Becoming an Orphan 241

Summing it Up 247

Filmography 255

The Eleanor Hunt Mystery 285

Index 289

About The Author 295

For Joycie

ACKNOWLEDGEMENTS

When I first contacted Joyce Compton in 1986 about answering some questions about her career, I had no idea it would lead to her putting her memories in print. She made it clear early on that she kept a lot of her thoughts inside.

She warned, "I've never been one to look back at the past or dwell on or talk about the old movie days to friends or anyone—unless they asked. To me, nothing is as boring as actors, long since out of the business and pitifully living in and talking about their past history. It seems so self-centered to keep on writing or talking of oneself. To tell a personal story, however, it's what has to be done."

Self reflection is a brave and often scary journey one takes, especially when writing your memories for public perusal and consumption and when the author is as private as Joyce Compton.

First and foremost, I thank Joyce for opening up her past for others to see. She recounts portions of her life that couldn't have been easy to relive. It was her intent, however, to not only share some of her Hollywood stories, but also to relate personal trials and disappointments. By her own admission, the process left her drained emotionally, physically, and spiritually.

I also thank Joyce's close friends, the late Bill and Norma Anderson, and their daughter, Judi, for their warm hospitality when I frequently journeyed to the West Coast during the '80s and '90s.

Special appreciation goes to writer Jim Parish, for his never-ending encouragement, and to silent film historian Roi Uselton, who continues to guide my research from the great beyond.

Thanks, Matt Hinrichs, for the use of a number of stills from his website, The Joyce Compton Shrine. Visit his site at *http://www.scrubbles.net/jc/bio.html.*

Finally, I'm forever grateful to Charlie Snipes and our girls, MaeBelle and Ms. Taylor.

A 1930s Joyce Compton glamour portrait.

PART I | *Biography and Interview*

It was only after knowing Joyce Compton for several years that I learned she had grown resentful of being referred to over the years as Hollywood's favorite dumb blonde. I made the mistake of using the moniker one too many times. Enough was enough. She told me so in a 1990 letter.

"I didn't shake the dumb blonde image after all. I could be referred to as a talented or favorite comedienne for a change," she wrote. "When writers say I played mainly waitresses or chorus girls, my fans and friends feel it is a putdown of my film roles. I can only recall one or two occasions of doing parts as a waitress and I never danced in films. The Southern and cute comedy roles prevailed among my work. Saying I was a favorite dumb blonde stands out like a sore thumb. It's worn threadbare."

I first approached Joyce in 1987 about an interview for *Classic Images*.[1] I was planning a trip to the West Coast in January 1988 and contacted her about the possibility of interviewing her about her long career that began in the mid-1920s. She agreed, but said she'd only consent to an interview by mail. In fact, she was adamant. "It will not be in person, and I do not go into all my frailties with fans, as it is discouraging to them," she explained. "They have the illusion, I think, that film personalities go on forever, looking and feeling as they did long ago. Not so. We all fade away as other mortals.

"One reason I won't do verbal interviews is because writers get things twisted or say what they want rather than what you've said. They even perpetuate stuff by copying information, sometimes incorrect, from other write-ups. The readers come away knowing nothing of my real personality and character, and are left with often dull and unimaginative stories."

Six months later, I was back in Los Angeles, and Joyce invited me to her home, Joycie's Hodge Podge Lodge, to meet and discuss plans for her memoirs that we decided to write together. She requested I come alone, "as it is hard for me to try and see strangers at this stage." She also warned, "You must not expect too much from me or my home. We are both worn out. It being 53 years old, and me, 81."

Joyce was a charming hostess that warm July day in 1988. She had treated me to a rare tour of the prized home she'd built and lived in for the past 50 years. I'd looked over her large memorabilia collection, studied her paintings (she was a gifted artist), and was now being led through her home that seemed haunted with memories of the past.

"This is where I used to sunbathe," the lady of the house said as she led her guest onto a well-hidden sun deck on the roof of her large Tudor-style home in Sherman Oaks.

---

[1] *Classic Images,* a monthly publication dedicated to classic films.

Gowns and furs she'd worn in her films and to parties and premieres filled her closets, and in her bedroom, was the sleigh bed she'd slept in for over half her life. Here a display of photographs, mostly of her fans, adorned her dresser, and letters from all over the world covered a small desk. This was her communication center, where she spent most of her time, writing to many film buffs who wanted to be in touch.

Joyce Compton and Michael G. Ankerich, July 1988.

Although Joyce reached out to the world through her mailbox, she was really a very private person and rarely invited the outside world into her private domain. Inside the walls of her Davana Street house, she lived in her own world, her sanctuary, in close communion with the one thing that had never let her down — her deep religious faith.

Joyce lived alone in this big house, alone except for Taj, her 16-year-old white Persian cat. Her mother and father, to whom she had been devoted all her life, had been dead for years. She was the last of what she referred to as "the team," her sometimes overly protective parents, and herself, an only child. For as long as she could remember, she'd been the breadwinner of the family, and she'd sometimes sacrificed a life of her own for the team. It was for the team that Joyce Compton lived and worked.

Over the next couple of years, Joyce pulled aside her curtain of secrecy and allowed me to see her private side. She insisted I call her Joycie, her nickname, the name her parents and friends had called her since childhood. The real Joyce Compton I came to know over the years was far from dumb. One of the screen's most gifted comediennes had another tale to tell, an incredible and often sad story.

BEGINNINGS

While many writers erroneously give her real name as Eleanor Hunt, she was actually born Olivia Joyce Compton[2] on January 27, 1907, in Lexington, Kentucky. When she was only a couple of months old, the family, her father, Henry, and her mother, Golden, moved to Gotebo, Oklahoma, to be near Joyce's Aunt Eula (Golden's sister), and her family. Joyce's earliest recollections are of Oklahoma and of being whisked into an underground cellar to escape tornados.

Joyce posing for the camera while still in Tulsa.

Joyce's father was a businessman who was always looking for an easy buck, the pot of gold at the end of the rainbow, wherever that might take his family. He would get wind of a business idea and move the family halfway across the country on a whim. From Oklahoma, the family moved to Idaho, Utah, Texas, Canada, and then back to Oklahoma, where they settled.

They remained in Oklahoma until the mid-1920s, when Joyce's father again became restless. He wanted to uproot the family and move to Florida, where a so-called real estate boom was unfolding. This time, however, Golden overruled her husband. She was not moving to Florida. If they moved anywhere, it would be California, where she had ideas about getting Joyce into the movies.

Joyce believed her mother had once wanted a stage or film career of her own and was now turning her sights to Joyce and was fulfilled living her dream through her daughter.

---

[2] For more information about the confusion over Joyce's name, refer to "The Eleanor Hunt Mystery," a later chapter in this book.

Joyce was in her teens by now and saw almost every movie that came to Tulsa. Snapshots of her at this time reveal a special beauty, even movie star looks, and neighbors and friends began to take notice.

HOLLYWOOD

In 1925, the Comptons sold their home in Oklahoma and struck out for California, their land of opportunity. They drove cross-country, sleeping in camp-grounds along the way to stardom.

After the family settled in the Los Angeles area, it wasn't long before cameras started rolling for Joyce. Golden saw an ad in the Los Angeles Examiner announcing a beauty contest for young hopefuls. She entered a beauty contest at the Ambassador Hotel. Picture people — directors, producers, and studio heads — served as judges. She easily won the first round and was sent to First National Studios for more interviews and screen tests. Again, she was a winner.

The night came when the winners were showcased in a program at Loew's State Theatre in downtown Los Angeles. The winners were asked to walk across the stage, bow to the audience, and take their cash prize. Joyce, a bit shy and over-whelmed by being in the spotlight, marched past the audience, took her check, and exited the stage. When she realized what she had done, there was no going back to take her bow. The show had gone on without her. She was devastated — and embarrassed. So shaken was she, that she exited the backstage door and took a streetcar home, leaving her parents in the theater. She collapsed in the porch swing and cried herself to sleep. Joyce was sure her career was over before she'd secured her first part.

During her first three months in Hollywood, Joyce stayed busy doing extra work. Then, she received her first studio call. She went to Vine Street in Hol-lywood, to the Famous Players-Lasky Studios, where she was an extra in the famous candy ball scene in Cecil B. DeMille's *The Golden Bed* (1925).

Working in pictures during those first months in Hollywood was just "like a big party all day," Joyce remembered telling her mother at the time. "The actors and actresses were just beautiful, glamorous people in an exciting, new world for me."

She was photographed with Rod La Rocque on the set of *The Golden Bed*, and saw such luminaries as Mae Murray, her favorite actress, walking across Hollywood Boulevard, and Rudolph Valentino, as he dined next to her and her mother.

Joyce was soon called to First National for a second round of interviews and possible work in films. "The director told me a few of the things he wanted me to do. I had no fear whatsoever. I was just totally natural, at ease. During the test, I threw my head back and puckered up my mouth and did my best Mae

Joyce was in Hollywood only a short time before the cameras started rolling.

Murray imitation." The test was a success, and Joyce signed a studio contract for $100 a week.

Her role in *What Fools Men* (1925), her first for First National, was a small one, but it captured the attention of critics. "One of the bright spots in the new First National film is the acting of youthful Joyce Compton," a critic wrote at the time.

Joyce Compton (background) in What Fools Men, *her first film for First National. Hugh Allan (right) is pictured with Shirley Mason and John Patrick.* COURTESY OF HUGH ALLAN.

Hugh Allan, cast as a chauffeur in the film, was signed at First National the same day as Joyce. He became her first Hollywood boyfriend. "Joyce was a delightful girl," Allan told me in 1992. "I was crazy about her. The studio always had us doing publicity, so one day, someone from the publicity department called and wanted us to be a best man and bridesmaid for a famous race car driver I had never heard of. They said the press would be there and it would be good for us." [3]

[3] Hugh Allan to Michael G. Ankerich, August 1992.

An early Joyce Compton portrait, mid-1920s.

Joyce was kept busy posing for publicity stills, making special appearances, and working in films such as *Syncopating Sue* (1926), with veteran actress Corinne Griffith, who, at this stage in her career, Joyce remembered as being rather difficult to work with.

Not only in *Syncopating Sue,* but in many of her silent films, Joyce found the older actresses were give special considerations for lighting and camera angles.

Corinne Griffith and Joyce (right) in Syncopating Sue *(1926).*

Joyce was oblivious to the politics involved in moviemaking.

Joyce's career was given momentum when she was designated one of 1926's Wampas Baby Stars, in the company of such budding actresses as Joan Crawford, Mary Astor, Janet Gaynor, Fay Wray, and Dolores Del Rio. "This was perhaps my biggest boost because of the worldwide publicity given that put us on the map as being film personalities and candidates for stardom," Joyce said.

Writer Roy Liebman, in his book, *The Wampas Baby Stars,* wrote that 1926 was the year that made the Wampas selectors look like they really did possess a crystal ball. "With such bright lights as Mary Astor, Joan Crawford, Dolores Del Rio, and Janet Gaynor it was positively luminescent. Even some of those who did not reach the superstar ranks, like Joyce Compton and Fay Wray, could be justly proud of their achievements." [4]

[4] Liebman, Roy. *The Wampas Baby Stars: A Biographical Dictionary, 1922-1934.* McFarland & Co., Jefferson, North Carolina, and London: 8

A mid-1920s portrait.

Not long after Joyce secured her First National contract, her father, never one to put down roots, decided to leave the family and pursue his original dream in Florida. Left without transportation, mother and daughter walked or rode streetcars to the studio.

About a year into her contact, First National, without notice, dropped Joyce's option. "I was thrown back into a cold, cruel, competitive Hollywood," she said.

Joyce was named one of the 1926 Wampas Baby Stars; (left to right) Dolores Costello, Vera Reynolds, Mary Astor, Marceline Day, Edna Marion, Mary Brian, Fay Wray, Janet Gaynor, Sally Long, Joyce Compton, Dolores Del Rio, Sally O'Neil, Joan Crawford.

"The studio heads assured me I was young yet and I'd be okay." Dad soon rejoined the family after his unsuccessful venture, and the three found themselves starting over again.

Working without a contract proved beneficial to Joyce. It was during this time that she did some of her best film work. Joyce was developing her own style of comedy and gaining a reputation at the studios as an effective comedienne and a cooperative and reliable professional.

Joyce made her talkie debut at Paramount in two Clara Bow vehicles: *The Wild Party* and *Dangerous Curves,* both 1929 releases. Since the studios were not yet equipped for sound, the shooting took place during the quiet hours of the night. Working all night was fine for some of the cast (like Bow), but the rigorous hours took their toll on Joyce.

"Filming these two early talkies was grueling, trying to get a crumb of sleep and rest at home during the day noises," she said. "My parents were concerned about my health holding out. Sure, I was young, but not very strong." Bow, on the other hand, was the opposite. "Clara was so strong and full of vitality. I was crazy about her."

In *The Wild Party*, a story of young flappers in a college dormitory, Joyce plays Eva Tutt, a student snoop who causes a college scandal when she tattles about the romance of her dorm mate (Bow) with the new anthropology professor (Fredric March).

Joyce as Eva Tutt in The Wild Party *(1929).*

After Joyce's two impressive performances in *The Wild Party* and *Dangerous Curves* (as a circus performer), Paramount offered Joyce a contract. By this time, however, Fox had offered her a nice role in *Salute* (1929), and Joyce turned down the Paramount deal.

FOX CHANGES JOYCE'S IMAGE

Salute, which revolved around the rivalry between Annapolis and West Point, took Joyce and the cast on location to Annapolis, Maryland.

Joyce said that director John Ford took special interest in her and did everything to protect her from the usual shenanigans that followed the crew on location.

Joyce and Charles Farrell, ca. 1929.

"I was very childlike then," she said, "probably from being such a sheltered family girl."

While she usually refrained from getting romantically involved with actors — she usually found them self-centered and egotistical — she found George O'Brien, the star of the picture, irresistible. "I did have a thing for him," she said, "but he seemingly didn't return the interest. He was a very polite gentleman and very careful of me. He was a solid man of standards and principles." Perhaps O'Brien was reluctant to get involved with an actress whose mother insisted on accompanying her daughter to the studio.

Back in Hollywood, following the filming of *Salute,* Joyce approached the heads of Fox Studios about more work. She liked working on *Salute* and decided she'd make a fine addition to their stable of actors.

The studio agreed and signed Joyce to a contract. The family's situation suddenly looked up in 1930. Joyce bought a baby grand piano, a fur coat, and new clothes. She and her parents rented a house in Benedict Canyon, directly below Rudolph Valentino's home, Falcon Lair, and around the corner from Jean Harlow and Paul Bern's residence.

The studio was interested in a Joyce Compton makeover. They dyed her hair and changed her makeup in hopes of giving her a more seductive, sensual image for the screen.

When Janet Gaynor was having problems at the studio and left for a short time, the studio began making plans to pair Joyce with Charles Farrell, Gaynor's co-star in such recent Fox hits as *7th Heaven* (1927), *Street Angel* (1928), and *Sunny Side Up* (1929).

Joyce's Fox makeover.

The two were photographed together and publicized as the studio's new romantic couple. Gaynor's differences with the studio were worked out and she returned to the studio. Joyce and Farrell were never teamed for the screen; instead, she went on location with Will Rogers and Joel McCrea to Lake Tahoe, Nevada, to film *Lightnin'* (1930).

Joyce and McCrea instantly hit it off. The two possessed the same values

Joyce cuddles with Ivan Lebedeff in Unholy Love *(1932).*

and standards, said Joyce, and had a natural attraction for the other. The relationship lasted only through the shooting of the picture, then it was back to Hollywood and more work. "We were both at the start of our careers, and all this kept us busy and pulling in opposite directions," she said. "Will Rogers noticed our budding relationship and told Joel to 'be careful of Red,' his nickname for me."

The Comptons were devastated when the Hollywood Savings and Loan collapsed. Joyce lost her life savings from motion pictures. Six months later, another blow was dealt the family when Fox Studios declined to renew Joyce's option.

"Here they had tried to change me to a more sophisticated type in appearance and otherwise by cutting and dyeing my hair. I thought they took me away from my natural appearance and comedy flair. Isn't that the way it goes? Sign you for what you have to offer, mess around and ruin it all, then give up and toss you out," Joyce said.

By the mid-1930s, Joyce's screen image (full of beauty, charm, and sugar) had been set.

JOYCE FINDS HER NICHE

Joyce went to New York on her first extended trip from her family to try to find work on the stage or screen. After three months of searching unsuccessfully for work, Joyce returned to Hollywood.

Although she worked only sporadically in silent films, at the advent of sound,

Joyce and Charley Chase share an intimate embrace in Manhattan Monkey Business.

after her disappointment at Fox, she had no trouble finding work. She soon cornered the market on dumb blondes, often applying her soft Southern accent to full comic relief. Returning to her blonde locks, she discovered a softer image that highlighted her charm and natural beauty.

The many film roles Joyce did in the 1930s were somewhat of a blur for her, unless the role stood out in importance. In later years, she left it to film researchers to sort out the specifics.

"I'm sure I haven't seen half the films I worked in. I often went to the dailies of the previous day's shooting in the studio's projection rooms. I'd see more of what I did before the cutting and I'd end up on the infamous cutting room floor."

For example, she played a beautician in *Beauty Parlor* (1932), a nurse in *Magnificent Obsession* (1935), a kept chorus girl in *Star for a Night* (1936), a Southern belle in *The Toast of New York* (1937), a drunken girl in *Kid Galahad* (1937), a vaudeville performer in *Artists and Models Abroad* (1938). There were many roles as girlfriends, chlorines, waitresses [*Mildred Pierce* (1945), for example], sometimes with lines that stole the scene.

COMEDIES AND WESTERNS

In 1933, Mack Sennett hired Joyce as an ingénue for his two-reel comedies. There, she made such films, as *Dream Stuff, Caliente Love, Daddy Knows Best, Knockout Kisses, The Plumber and the Lady,* and *Roadhouse Queen.* She remembered the Mack Sennett Studios as being rather unorganized and chaotic.

Joyce and Walter Pidgeon embrace in Sky Murder *(1940).*

After working for Mack Sennett, Joyce was foil to such comedians as Bobby Clark and Paul McCullough (*Everything's Ducky* at RKO was a popular film) and Charley Chase, in such comedies as *Life Hesitates at 40, Public Ghost No. 1,* and *Manhattan Monkey Business* at Hal Roach's studio).

The comedy roles were among her favorites. "I enjoyed those roles, for I could put my own unique touch into the character instead of just playing straight or dramatic roles," she said. "I was best suited for comedy."

In 1934 and 1935, Joyce made 11 features and a 12-chapter Western serial, *Rustlers of Red Dog* (1935), with Johnny Mack Brown. Western file buffs also remember Joyce for other Westerns, such as *Border Cavalier* (1927) with Fred Hume, *Fighting for Justice* (1932), *Valley of the Lawless* (1936) with Johnny Mack Brown, and *Silver Spurs* (1943).

Joyce often complained that working in short subjects and Westerns gave her little to do but stand around and look pretty, while the comedians and cowboys got the laughs and cheers.

Joyce in her "Gone with the Wind" dress in The Awful Truth *(1937).*

PERSONAL FAVORITES

It was when she started freelancing again in the mid-1930s that her career advanced with better roles in first-rate films. They became some of her personal favorites.

In *The White Parade* (1934), Joyce plays Una Mellon, one of six student nurses (one being Loretta Young) in a nursing school. She plays a matchmaking sister of Maureen O'Sullivan in *Spring Madness* (1937), and a detective who, with Walter Pidgeon, investigates the murder of a polo star.

Joyce's best role came in 1937 when she played Dixie, a café singer and Cary Grant's girlfriend, in *The Awful Truth*. Grant is overcome with embarrassment when his ex-wife, played by Irene Dunne, brings her new boyfriend to the club where Joyce is performing. Dunne arrives just in time to see her sing her number called "Gone with the Wind," during which her dress blows over her head when she sings the line, "My dreams are gone with wind."

A NEW DIRECTION

Joyce worked steadily throughout the 1940s. Some roles were more substantial than others. She was particularly fond of her work in *Turnabout* (1940), *Christmas in Connecticut* (1945), and *A Southern Yankee* (1948). Some parts were little more than bits [*Mildred Pierce* (1945) and *Sorry, Wrong Number*

Dennis Morgan and Joyce in Christmas in Connecticut *(1945).*

(1948), for example]. She switched to occasional work in television in the 1950s.

By the end of the 1940s, with fewer calls for film work, Joyce began looking for a new direction in her life. She found, however, that she wasn't trained nor had she any experience in anything but motion pictures.

Her mother's declining health in the early 1950s took much of her attention. Golden's death in 1953 gave Joyce the idea for a second career. "Mom's doctors thought I was an excellent nurse, and knowing I sought a new career, started recommending and calling me to help on some of their home cases. So my training as a nurse came through personal experience and the doctors' instructions. I was doing something worthwhile for others, and each case was different and a new challenge."

Her patients had fun with the fact that Joyce had once been a movie actress who still had occasional parts in films and on TV. "They recognized the name beforehand and wondered if I was *the* Joyce Compton. I would take my movie stills with me and tell them my Hollywood stories, and this would take their minds off their troubles for a little while. I guess you could say I was still in the entertainment business."

A BRIEF MARRIAGE

Devoted to her overprotective parents, Joyce had never developed a serious relationship. She lived with her parents in the house they built together in 1935. Even as an adult, Joyce would often have to sneak out of the house if she wanted a night on the town.

Three years after her mother's death, in 1955, Joyce married William "Bill" F. Kahiler, a Long Beach jeweler, at the Hollywood Presbyterian Church. Alisa Guard, a Hungarian actress, served as Joyce's matron of honor. The couple lived in the groom's home for a short time before they separated. The marriage was annulled in February, 1956. Joyce returned to live with her dad.

In the early 1960s, her father's physical and mental health began to fail. He suffered a nervous breakdown and was in and out of institutions before he died in 1965. With his death, Joyce said, "I became an orphan." She left films for good, quit her nursing career, rented out part of her house, and got some much-needed rest.

For her 35-year career in motion pictures, which consisted of an estimated 200 film appearances, Joyce was honored in the late 1960s with a star on Hollywood Boulevard.

LATER YEARS

When I contacted Joyce in 1986, she was spending her final years at the home she'd built with her parents. She tended to housework and took care of her cat, Taj. What maintenance needs she couldn't attend to went undone. It was a lonely existence for her at this point. Having no children or close kin, Joyce would sometimes send herself Mother's Day cards from Taj.

In 1989, after completing her memoirs, Joyce's health began to decline. She suffered a stroke in early September. On September 22, she wrote to let me know.

> *Brief word from Joycie. Sept. 1 — Collapsed in yard with stroke. Lay on ground helpless. Two hours alone. Right leg and arm struck out, useless. Screaming. No one to hear or find me. God finally helped a bit, enabled me to scoot backwards on ground to the back door. In course of events, was in Motion Picture Hospital intensive care. Days and*

nights of a nightmare of endless tests. After many horror events, I am home trying to make it. Taking care of self and Taj. He had a time, too.

In early 1990, she suffered a series falls and heart scares. She struggled with high blood pressure, skin cancer, arthritis in her feet and legs, poor circulation, and bone spurs. She began to contemplate a move to a healthcare facility. In one letter she wrote, "I'm hoping and praying for God's release to come before such drastic undertakings."

Joyce scraped by on $350 a month from Social Security. She complained that her beloved home, now surrounded by a jungle of trees and plants she couldn't tend, was falling into disrepair around her. Bees built a hive in the walls of her bedroom to which she now confined herself. The winter of 1990 was especially tough for her and Taj. She wrote:

It's so very cold. I put on two or three of everything: socks, slacks, sweaters, robes, and get on a heating pad. I put a little jacket on Taj and cover him with his little blankets. He leans against his heater in the bathroom. I only heat my bedroom and his area. It would cost a few hundred per month to gas heat this big barn of a house.

By May of 1990, Joyce decided she couldn't go on alone. Using an inner strength she had drawn on in times of crisis, she sold her home, had her vet put Taj to sleep, and checked herself into the Motion Picture and Television Country Hospital in Woodland Hills, CA.

She wrote on July 31, 1990:

It seems my whole past — home, all possessions — has been wiped out over night. Little Taj is in kitty land. I'm in a different world now. There was nothing left for me at home. Not another day. I barely made it to the hospital to drop into bed, where I've been for the past two months. Strange, the turns of events that has happened in my life. I'm without a trace of the past 55 years in my home. It seems there comes a time in our latter days, when all we may need or have left is an adjustable bed, tray meals, medication, and a few people around to help us. I have a cubicle area with two drawers and drapes separating me from another ill patient. My world!

Although she took art classes at the Motion Picture Home, she found it difficult to adjust to being around others. "Bingo, sing-a-longs, and movies they show are not for me," she said when I visited her in March 1991. "I feel more like an inmate than a resident. There's nothing but rows and rows of white-haired horrors. I could crawl the walls with nerves. I'm a changed person. Not much is left of the old me that was. I'm at the end of my road for sure."

Joyce died October 13, 1997, at the Motion Picture Hospital. She was 90. Following a graveside service that was conducted by her closest friends, Norma Anderson and Judi Morris, Joyce was buried in Forest Lawn Hollywood Hills Cemetery.

Joyce's star on Hollywood Boulevard.

I found Joyce, in contrast to the many simple-minded roles she played on the screen, to be a complicated individual and a deep thinker. To her mother years before, she described herself another way. "I have a young body, a sad heart, and an old soul. I don't mean a reincarnated soul, but more of a serious or spiritual depth to my inner personality than my cheerful, perky, youthful, or comedic exterior gave forth."

While she often portrayed dumb blondes on the screen, she was no dummy. As Joyce once told writer Leonard Maltin, "Sometimes one has to be smart to play dumb." [5]

She developed into one of the screen's finest and most versatile comediennes by using her natural talent and personality. "Comedy was a natural flair and part of who I was," Joyce said. "I have a great sense of humor and enjoy making people laugh and be happy. I laugh a lot. After all, laughing makes better wrinkles."

[5] Maltin, Leonard. *The Reel Stars.* Curtis Books, 1973.

Joyce Compton, ca 1929.

PART II | *A Note on the Memoir*

Joyce Compton revived the idea of writing her memoir during the interview we did in 1988. She had actually toyed for years with the idea of putting her memories on paper, even purchasing a copy of *Writer's Digest* to explore the market.

As she was celebrating her 81st birthday on January 27, 1988, she took a break from writing responses to my questions and wrote a letter asking about the possibility of me helping her tell her story.

> *Mike, it seems we have so much material here. I keep thinking that we practically have an autobiography. It seems a shame to give it to one little article. Would there be a possibility of us turning all this information into something more worthwhile? Could we interest a book publisher? I have some ambitions about what we might accomplish for us both. I would write the story and you would arrange and hang it all together. I won't be here much longer, so now would have to be our opportunity.*
>
> *People who like the films and stars of that era, from the 1920s on through the 1950s, I think, would like to have such a personally-written account of some of the highlights of an actress's life. Most everyone pictures us all as rich and famous and never hear of another side.*
>
> *I've even thought of the title:* The Real Joyce Compton: Behind the Dumb Blonde Movie Image.
>
> *Sound good? It's a thought.*

For the next six months or so, from January to June 1988, Joyce put her story on paper. She set a rather strict routine for herself. She wrote in longhand, often propped up in bed. When she finished a chapter, she drove to a local Kinkos to copy the pages, then to her local post office. It was an arduous task for her, one that grew more so as the process continued.

At one point, she wondered whether I would be the only one interested in the story of her life. She wrote:

> *I wonder, while knocking myself out with writing my stuff, whether anyone will be interested in the real Joyce Compton or only the movie image. Will they turn away from my serious side? Maybe I'm sounding negative, but I'm more of a fact facer than a dreamer, I think. That's one reason I've never*

Page from Joyce's handwritten manuscript.

pursued wasting my time writing or struggling to find an art outlet other than decorating my home.

In the middle of the writing, her strength began to ebb. She made it clear that her participation in our project was limited to completing the draft.

I need to let you know that no way could I ever promote a book by traveling or making appearances, giving interviews, meeting people, or autographing books. I'll be lucky just to finish the draft to leave behind. Then, I'll be ready to move out of this body and be at peace to forget my past careers, this life — all of it — and be ready to start that whole new afterlife.

Always a trooper, Joyce forged ahead with the project. By June, she'd relived her life and came through the experience exhausted.

Who writes a book in five months? It has been a hard push for me all these months. I've hurried through my writing in fear I might give out and not be able to complete my story.

I've been writing long hours for five months. My eyeballs are falling out. My brain is closing down, saying, "Enough!"

Throughout 1988, I approached publishers with the idea. Most said, through form letters, that the book was not for them. Joyce never wanted to see the rejection slips or involve herself in the details. After an aggressive effort, we were unable to find a publisher for our project. It was disappointing for both of us, but was especially devastating for Joyce.

I moved on to interviewing other silent film stars for a couple of books I published in the 1990s. Perhaps it was not the right time for Joyce's story. It seems that now, 20 years later, as interest in classic films continues to grow, it is the time to tell the story of one of the most fascinating character actresses the screen has known.

PART III

Behind the Dumb Blonde Movie Image

CHAPTER I | *My Beginnings*

It was a cold, blustery, stormy night when Henry ran stumbling through the deep snow to get the doctor for his wife, Golden. Her time had come. On arriving, the doctor took one look at her, went over and sat by the big stove, while Golden pulled on the bedpost to help her delivery. About 6 a.m., on January 27, 1907, in Lexington, Kentucky, I came forth to take my chances in the world. The doc tied the cord, pronounced me a girl, and collected his $5 fee. My parents were left with Olivia Joyce Compton to raise and cherish.

Some months later, Mom coaxed Dad to take our family to Gotebo, Oklahoma, where her sister, my aunt Eula, and husband, Uncle Clen, had gone to work in the oil fields. They were drilling for the black gold.

We were planted there on the flat plains with the tumbleweeds whirling across the prairies, a place where cyclones and tornados ripped into town frightening everyone into storm caves and leaving strange things and havoc in their wake.

My earliest recollections are of being whisked at night down into our underground cellar. A tornado had touched down and we were in its path. We'd sit there in the candlelight until

Me and my beloved mother.

we dared check to see if the horror had passed and had left our house intact. Remember *The Wind?* What we endured on the plains was not unlike what Lillian Gish experienced in that silent classic.

Above ground, where the storm cave was built, was a high dirt mound. It was my joy to race over this dirt. Putting my cat in my go-cart, I'd push back and forth over the mound until my Dad would say to Mom, "Must she do this? She's wearing all the dirt off the boarding beneath."

I suspect I also wore a path with my go-cart from our house across the prairie to Aunt Eula's, where Mom often wheeled me along.

Hearing a tornado had been sighted and coming our way, Mom would wrap a blanket around me and stand me behind a door while she hurried to get clothes off the line and shut the windows. She always warned that if two windows were open, the winds would pass through the house, lift the foundation, and set us down somewhere else.

Winds were fierce out on the prairie. I wore those rolled-brim Buster Brown hats over my long golden curls. Crossing the weeded plain, the winds would catch my hat, whisk it off into the air, and roll it over and over like a tumbleweed. I would cry out in exasperation, "Mama, I just can't keep that hat on to save my life."

Little Joycie at age 2.

When I was about two, I picked up some kind of intestinal condition and wasn't expected to live. Mom told me later she stayed on her knees by her bed all night, praying and asking the Lord to spare me. If spared, she said, she would give me over. The next morning, I was much improved.

I remember frequent visits to Aunt Eula's. She had a big wood stove that burned all day. Uncle Clen's old hound dog, Bob, used to lie sprawled out in front of the stove until called to go hunting. "Bob" was the first word I learned to say. Uncle Clen would go quail hunting with ole Bob in the dark morning and come in later with a string of quail for dinner. Breakfast was often chicken fried steak, cream gravy, hot biscuits or corn meal cakes made in the skillet.

Uncle Clen's pet name for Eula was "Tootsie," so I often called her Aunt Tootsie. She would talk of wanting to have a child of her own. Clen would tell her, "Tootsie, you would be about as big as a minute with a baby." I suspect it would have been too much for her frail body. They never had children of their own.

Mom went out of town once and left me with Aunt Eula. I stood for days looking for Mom through the lace curtains over the oval glass of the front door. I listened intently for the train whistle in the distance and looked with such longing to see Mom coming across the flat land. When she finally arrived, Aunt Eula said, "Golden, don't ever go away and leave that child alone again. She has stood at that door looking and longing in such loneliness that there was nothing I could do to comfort her." Mom and I always had a strong bond.

When I was four, we went to live in Spokane, Washington, where we rented a large two-story house. The big snows, apple festivals, and playing in the grove of pines next door are what I most remember about Spokane. I was able to walk by myself to the store for the first time. With Mom's note and some change in my hand for the grocery man, I'd take a few steps and look back at Mom on the porch.

From Spokane, we moved on to Boise City, Idaho. Then, it was Salt Lake City, Utah. We seemed always to be moving. Dad tried new business ventures and Mom and I usually went along. I just wanted to be settled, so I could make friends with our neighbors and schoolmates.

My Uncle Clen and Aunt Eula.

Somewhere along the way, my grandmother, Mom's mother from Kentucky, came to live with us. She had been widowed and didn't find a happy home in Kentucky with her son and family. Once, Mom, Grandma, and I took a trip to visit Aunt Geneva and Uncle Alvin, Mom's brother, and their five children. They lived on a large farm outside Louisville, Kentucky.

I was excited to see my first farm and some of my relatives. Getting to the two-story house, I ran ahead of everyone, opened the front door, and exclaimed, "We're here!" I didn't know any of them, had never met them, because I was growing up all over the country.

A lady, I suppose it was Aunt Geneva, came hurrying down the stairs. It seemed there was a child on every step coming down behind her.

I remember big feather mattresses on the beds and pitchers and bowls to wash in. Also, there were tall pots with lids and smaller chambers for under the beds. There were wooden toilets at a distance out back. Two of them even had three holes. There were old catalogs for tissue paper and spiders and cobwebs in the upper corners of the small building. It seemed strange to me, as I had lived in cities during our travels around the country.

I had a great time playing with all the cousins, but at the same time, it was awkward. We were so different from each other. It seemed I was more advanced. I think being taught at home and in schools around the country was the difference. Also, I was so neat and clean, while my cousins were haphazard in dress. They couldn't spell and, in many ways, were way behind in learning. My aunt and uncle took note of this and marveled at the comparison, feeling somewhat ashamed of their own brood.

We landed in Dallas, Texas, when I was seven. When I look back, I'd say this was the time in our lives when we were really rich. I remember a big Christmas with lots of toys and Dad playing with toys and spinning the tops. Because of my advancement, probably from being taught at home, I was placed directly in the second grade.

About the time we moved to Dallas.

After school, I dragged all the poor waifs home to play with my dolls and toys and to see my paper dolls and all the clothes I'd made for them. I trace my talent for clothes designing back to these days of making paper doll clothes. I once brought home a bedraggled looking child who stuttered. Mom called me in and shoved the little girl away, for fear I'd catch the condition.

From Dallas, we moved to Toronto, Canada, a seemingly foreign land to me. After awhile, we returned to the States. There was Kansas City and various small towns in Oklahoma. I was always getting acquainted with new schools and making new friends. I longed to be anchored in a home of our own.

I was eight or nine when we finally settled in Tulsa, Oklahoma. This was a little house we actually bought, not rented. Dad lived mostly out of town, trying to find work in other places. He sometimes sold oil leases or drilled with partners. Then, he had a Spavinaw Lake realty project, which kept him home enough for us to camp on the lake. I loved the outdoors, fishing in the streams, and wearing my khaki gym bloomers. Soon, however, Dad was off again to find greener pastures, leaving Grandma, Mom, and me alone.

Conditions eventually became financially rough for us. Dad wasn't able to send much money for us to live on. We had some credit at the market and Mom planted our whole backyard with a vegetable garden. We stored the potatoes and canned the vegetables. With a little meat from the market, we made out until Dad could send a few dollars.

During World War I, people needed rentals and roofs over their head. Again, Mom put together a plan to help our situation by renting our house for $90 a month. It seemed like a fortune at the time. Mom put up a makeshift bedroom with three cots in the small basement where we kept our canned food. Mom, Grandma, and I slept there, but we kept the bathroom and kitchen privileges for us. When our boarders were finished with their cooking and meals, we climbed the stairs to the kitchen and prepared our food.

While times were tough, those lean days didn't seem so bad. We just went along, doing what had to be done to survive. I went to school and didn't seem to be unhappy or worried about anything.

CHAPTER 2 | *A Death in the Family*

Grandma developed what they called a leakage in her heart and wasn't expected to live. In time, she went to stay with Aunt Eula. The call came that Grandma had little time left. Mom and I went to the small oil town where they lived. Grandma's two sons, Baptist preachers from Kentucky, came to bid farewell to their mother.

The folks hovered around Grandma for what seemed like days. I tried to entertain myself outside away from the adults. I was outside playing in a pair of Uncle Clen's hunting boots when I heard the weeping. Grandma was gone. I struggled to get the boots off my feet and ran to see what was happening. By the time I got in, they had pulled the sheet over her face and were moaning softly and comforting each other.

Grandma was a wonderful Christian lady with a storybook past of living as a child through the Civil War in the South. She brought up her children in the fear and admonition of the Lord. In Kentucky, with so much whiskey-making and feuding going on, she made her children sign pledges not to drink, smoke, or play cards.

At the family gathering, I heard them talking about Grandma's last moments. It seemed she kept pointing upwards. Was she referring to the paper shading around the ceiling light? She shook her head, not able to speak, but still pointing with a rapt expression on her face. It was decided she saw the angels that had come to take her home.

When Grandma was all dressed up and in the casket in the corner of the living room, I stood close looking at her. It was my first sight of a dead body. She looked so sweet and peaceful lying there in her white silk gloves.

CHAPTER 3

Discovering the Facts of Life and Other Teenage Difficulties

My family belonged to the Boston Avenue Methodist Church, where I was always in Sunday school. Some of the girls had learned to flirt with the boys. We were learning fast that boys were different from us. If we sat on top of the sloped seats in Sunday school, we could see over the curtain and peep and giggle at the boys across the room. Our misbehavior was distracting and often drove our teacher to exasperation.

Donald and Bob, two brothers who lived next door to us, also began to realize that girls were different. They would make wooden swords and, using their mother's boiler lids, fight duels over me. They would run, then kneel at my feet. I was already playing the damsel in distress or the heroine needing to be rescued.

One day, I saw a strange sight. Two of our neighborhood dogs were joined together in a rather funny way. After watching awhile, I ran and called Donald and Bob to come and have a look. They were already wise to what was going on. Instead of teasing or mocking me, they told me that, sometime later, the female would have some baby puppies. Sure enough, one day while playing in some tall weeds, I heard some whimpering. There, in the brush, was the mother and her pups. That was my introduction to the facts of life.

Katy, another school chum, had an older sister who had just gotten married. She told some of the little girls what went on after marriage on their wedding night. Katy was always telling lies, so I thought it was all ridiculous and didn't believe a word of it.

I began seeing some of the older girls in dark places with the boys. They were kissing pretty heavily. It all looked so mysterious to me.

Then, there was Bernice who lived on the corner. Her parents worked, which meant she was home alone after school. Irving, on his way back from the springs to get a pail of water, would stop to visit Bernice. The dogs would come by and lap the water. Finally, Irving would come out, get his pail, and be on his way home. Other boys also came to see Bernice. The neighborhood whisperings started.

Dad finally told me I couldn't play with or go to Bernice's house. He gave no explanation and I couldn't understand why. Bernice and I had always been friends. I went anyway. Of course, he caught me, took me home and spanked me. It was the only spanking he ever gave me.

Bernice and her family were shunned by the neighbors. It seemed so sad for me to see Bernice walking alone up the street and not being able to say anything to her. Sometime later, Bernice became very sick. Mom told me Bernice had gotten pregnant and aborted the baby. I was learning some sad facts of life.

Mom always allowed the boys to freely visit our house. There was no slipping around. She was their friend and liked to talk to them. The boys liked her and felt at home. When boys first came to visit, they'd bring me packages of gum and jawbreakers.

When I was older, as a teenager, my suitor would bring me a box of candy and we would sit on the porch swing and talk. Donald and Bob, the neighborhood boys, couldn't understand why they shouldn't move in on me and my date and help eat the candy. After all, I was like one of the boys they'd grown up with. Mom would tactfully call them into the house and explain that this was different and that they couldn't barge in on my date.

A "long pants" boy, older than my teen friends, the knickers crowd, came to visit. We would go out with our dates on a Sunday afternoon with our Kodak cameras and take pictures of ourselves. Suddenly, the fellow dropped out of sight. I called and wanted to know why. He said he didn't love me anymore. I was devastated and threw myself on the bed in a weeping drama. Mom was concerned until she found nothing serious had happened to me. The young man was just too mature to be dating the child that I still was with my long curls and ruffled dresses. He gave me my first broken heart, but I survived!

One night, a long-distance call came from Uncle Clen. Aunt Eula, Mom's sister, was seriously ill with flu. He asked if we could send a nurse, as they had none in their little town. Mom did and Eula seemed to improve. The nurse left too soon, for Eula became too weak to be up on her own. The call came that Aunt Eula had passed away. Again, Mom and I left Tulsa to attend a family funeral.

Uncle Clen met us at the train station. We made it to the little country house in the early dawn light. A window was open and the curtains floated eerily in and out with the light breeze. I could see the corner of the gray coffin. In the distance, a rooster crowed. A new day was beginning.

We went in to find a couple of neighbors were sitting with the body. There lay Aunt Eula looking like so gray and gaunt. She reminded me of a piece of clay. Aunt Eula's death was a very sad loss for us. She was only forty. Her life was over too soon.

Sometime after Aunt Eula's death, Mom surprised me with the news that she was expecting a baby. I was quite excited about the possibility of having a little brother or sister. I started making plans, one of which was to knit a baby cap for the newcomer. After only a few months, however, Mom miscarried and lost the baby. This had been one of several miscarriages she'd had over the years. It turned out that I was the only child she could have.

Mom had a lot of physical problems after her last miscarriage. She was in bed a lot and had to stay off her feet. I would come home at noon from school to check on her and fix her lunch.

Dad was away, as usual, so I was her only help now that Grandma and Aunt Eula were gone. I look back across these over 70 years and remember how lonely I felt and so responsible for my mother's well being. I had no one to lean on or help me. It was quite a load of responsibility for a mere teenager.

Mom didn't improve for a long time. She wasn't getting any better and it was obvious she couldn't go on with her condition. The doctors decided on a hysterectomy. Thankfully, Mom's brother came to be with us through the surgery.

I remember sitting on the steps of the hospital in Tulsa and feeling so lonely and helpless. I prayed to God to spare my only mother. There was little nursing help in the hospital, as I remember, unless one had the financial means to hire a private nurse, so Uncle Raymond would go over and sit by her side through the long nights.

Dad made it back to town in time to pay the hospital bill. Then, he was off again, and it was just Mom and me.

Over time, Mom's strength improved. As I continued to mature, I began to notice and enjoy the attentions of the opposite sex. Some of the bolder boys were starting to push me against the front porch wall for closer contact and a kiss or two.

After my dates, Mom would wait up to hear how they went. I'd had my long curls bobbed by then and the upper part needed tighter curling. Mom got a lot of rag strips, and as I sat on the floor between her knees, she would roll my hair and tie the rags. She would get the milk

11-year-old Joycie looking rather studious.

and cookies and I sit there and tell her everything that happened. That's how close we were.

I'd show her my love letters, and Mom was right there helping me write the answers. She looked forward to reading those little love notes as much as I did. Mom seemed to be reliving her girlhood through me. We were being young together.

As I got older, I spent more and more time at the movies. One time, I came out of the theatre into the dark night and realized I'd spent all my change. I had no money for car fare. I was facing a long walk home in the dark. I can still see that lonely viaduct along the way that crossed over some railroad tracks. Houses were sparse and few cars came that way.

I was sort of dressed up. Mom had taken some of Aunt Eula's clothes and tailored them for me. I had on a little suit and a big movie star hat that made me look much older and more sophisticated than I was.

As I walked along, I became aware of a car following me. It came closer and I realized there were two men in the front seat. One jumped out and came up to me. I just clenched my fists and flipped on by. He went back to the car. I thought I had scared them off. I got to the bridge and hurried across to find them waiting on the other side. They again moved in on me.

One man got out and seemed determined to stop me and pull me into the car with him. Thankfully, I saw two people walking toward me and that scared the men away. I ran a few more blocks home to find Mom waiting for me on the front porch. She was frantic with worry.

Mom had premonitions about things and knew I was in danger. I'd like to think her prayers scared those men away and brought the people along at the right moment. It was a dangerous world, even in those days. When I went to the movies from then on, I was careful not to become so lost in those flickering images that I lost track of what was going on in the real world around me.

CHAPTER 4 | *Hollywood, Here I Come!*

In early 1925, Dad, ever on the hunt for greener pastures and new business ventures, got the urge to make another move in our lives. He was thinking Florida this time and hung a large map on the wall to study the driving route we would take. He had heard there was an expected boom in real estate.

I was 18 by now and enjoyed going to the movies quite a bit. I had a boyfriend or two who worked as ushers at the neighbor theater, and they would let me in for free. I must have seen every film that played in Tulsa.

Photos showed that I was photogenic and people began to notice my appearance. Some commented on what a cute profile I had. I hardly knew what a profile was. But, I got a mirror and, getting close to the dresser mirror, I had a look at mine. It seemed okay. I thought I had a nice nose.

Mom was also taking note of my assets and began to think Hollywood and the movies. She often talked to me about it and asked me what I thought. I think she had felt the insecurity of Dad's unstable business ventures and wanted to plan some kind of a secure future for me. I would listen to her and get excited. The

Imitating a Sennett Bathing Beauty while still in Tulsa.

more she talked, the closer I studied the movies I was seeing.

I liked the Mae Murray type and would look in the mirror and practice her look: thrown-back head, droopy eyes, and bee-stung pucker. I thought I could be that type. Then again, with my long, golden curls, I might be a Mary Pickford or even a Lillian Gish, with a wistful, child-like look.

As Dad continued talking Florida, Mom began actively proposing Hollywood, saying, "We've had our chance, Henry. Let's go to Hollywood and see if we can give our Joycie an opportunity in the movies. You can always try your luck out there."

To our surprise, Dad agreed. He now went about plotting how to get us there. While used to traveling solo, he now had Mom and me in tow.

Dad loved cars, and we always seemed to have several sitting around. One of them was a Winton 6, an open touring car that had fastening Isenglass curtains and a big running board. It was as big as Noah's Ark. This car was really spectacular in those days and men were always coming around to look under the hood.

On a few occasions, Mom had gotten Dad to leave the keys to that big car when he left town. Although she didn't drive, we would get a trustworthy neighbor boy to drive us around. I would get some of my pals to come along and we would take off across town. Maple Ridge was the Beverly Hills of Tulsa, and we

On our way to Hollywood.

would see all the rich folk's homes. The boys let me steer a bit and taught me how to shift gears. My first driving lesson and we lived to tell about it!

Dad chose this stunning Winton 6 car for our long trip to California. We sold the house and all the furniture, keeping only the upright player piano and Dad's music rolls. They were shipped after we settled in our new home.

Mom put all my pretty dresses she made in suit boxes and stacked them by her on the backseat. She made herself a khaki skirt and sewed the little diamond ring Aunt Eula had left me in the hem for safekeeping. We tied our last possessions to the running board: pots and pans, a big iron skillet, and a Sterno heater. We planned to camp all the way to Los Angeles.

I put on my middy blouse and gym bloomers, and the Comptons were off for California! We looked like the Beverly Hillbillies, no doubt. But, we were young and off to new adventures.

We left for California very early one morning. I remember seeing a neighbor standing on her porch and waving goodbye to us. My best beau at the time had asked to drive in escort with us as far as Oklahoma City. He admonished me to come back with him and "look after his interest." He further warned, "I hear that the makeup they use out there eats holes in your skin!"

We traveled in the flatland of Oklahoma forever, it seemed. We saw mountains in the distance that would take days and days to reach. We finally came to the beautiful pines of Flagstaff, Arizona. We found a campground and stayed there for several weeks to rest from our travels.

Dad got out the big tent and poles he'd packed away. It was a large tarpaulin that covered the car and extended on either side. There, Mom and I, with our folding Army cots, had sleeping accommodations. Dad made himself a stretcher bed that rested from back of the car across the front seat.

We got the tent up just before the rains came. Oh, how it poured! We thought we would drown in the rain and mud. Mom and I crawled in the big car and helped Dad fasten up the Isenglass curtains. We got in together and stayed dry and cozy.

There was a recreation hall in the center of the campground. We wandered down there one evening and peeped in the windows to see young people dancing and having fun. A young boy spied me, came outside, and asked me to dance. I was not suitably dressed. So Mom, as understanding as ever, took me back to our car and looked in the suit boxes until she found one of my cute dresses. I went back to the dance, joined the crowd, and danced with my new admirer.

The next day, he took me to his home to meet his mother. I took some dresses with me to press so I'd have some neat clothes to wear when we got to Los Angeles. He was definitely smitten and made me promise to write when we got to Hollywood.

Our journey continued and the terrain soon turned to desert. In the middle of the Mojave Desert, our car broke down. We were stranded by a lone filling station along the highway. Dad, needing a certain part for the repair, caught a bus and went ahead of us to buy the part. We had no idea when he would return. Mom and I were quite alone, sitting by the side of the road in that open car. We must have looked a sight!

It was hot, but bearable during the day. At night, when the station attendant went home and closed the station, we were both scared to death.

One day, a car carrying several rough men drove up. They hung around the station and started talking to Mom and me. Their eyes were on me, of course. They didn't seem to be in a hurry to move on. We were really uneasy and tried not to be too friendly with them, letting them know that Dad would be back any minute.

He did return, and when the car was repaired, we were on our way. On the outskirts of Los Angeles, we stopped at some fruit stands and bought a bucket of oranges for a quarter. What a treat! In Oklahoma, an orange had been like a box of candy at Christmas.

When we got into Los Angeles, we stayed with some friends we knew in the Glendale area. They had a daughter about my age and invited me to stay with them until my folks found a place for us. Mom and Dad went on to a Santa Monica campground overlooking the big Pacific Ocean. They rested there and used the campground as their base while they looked around for a house we could rent. All the money we had was whatever our small house in Tulsa had sold for. We were certainly taking a gamble on little ole Joycie.

Mom and Dad picked me up a couple of weeks later to go down to the campground and see that vast ocean. I gasped at such a wide expanse of water.

We stayed at the campground, which turned out to be near the Santa Monica Pier. It had a big dance pavilion called the La Monica Ball Room and was all set up for entertainment. I got dressed up and went there in the evenings with my folks. So, whomever I met had to meet the parents as well. It was all safe. I had an admirer right off the bat, a sweet young lad with an open roadster.

In looking for a rental we could afford, Dad drove us around the San Fernando Valley. Who would have thought I was destined to build my home there much later and be there over the next 50 years?

CHAPTER 5 | *My Break into the Movies*

I was in sunny California. I'd get buckets of oranges, squeeze the pitcher full of juice, play my ukulele, and sing to my heart's content. There was not a care in the world. Dad got a job selling tires with an old friend he had previously known and I set my eyes on becoming an actress.

Mom insisted we be in the heart of Hollywood, so we could get to studio and casting offices using the streetcars. After all, that's what we were here for. We needed to be in the middle of the action. We found a little duplex on North Hobart Avenue, a side street near Western Avenue and Santa Monica Boulevard. Street cars went in all directions. Two elderly ladies owned the place and lived in the other side. There was a nice yard out back and a big canopy swing.

It was not long after we arrived in Hollywood that I got a glimpse of my favorite movie star, the one I'd seen only in the dark movie theaters back in Tulsa, the one I'd imitated in the mirror. There she was, Mae Murray, crossing Hollywood Boulevard on foot in a large picture hat and lacy black hose looking rather flamboyant for the street. Wow! There was no doubt that I was in Hollywood, ready to make my entrance.

About the same time, Mom and I went to lunch at a famous and popular place on Hollywood Boulevard where all the stars frequented. They would be ushered upstairs. Everyone waited until the maitre d' recognized you and motioned you to your table. Aside from the tables in the middle of the room, instead of booths, there was seating circling the walls, so that everyone was sitting close to the next person. You could see what they ate, hear their conversation, and so on. Not very private! One day for luncheon, we were seated right next to Rudolph Valentino and some of his friends. He was eating spaghetti. Mom and I were very sophisticated and nonchalant. We didn't dare glare at him or appear to even be aware of him, much less butt in like peasants or ask for an autograph. Rudy was quite a colorful character in his time and one of my favorites!

When not stargazing, Mom took me to a photographer and had some cute photos made. I was 17, but looked more like 12 or 13.

Before we could turn around to make our next move, Dad came in with the Los Angeles Herald-Examiner and pronounced, "Well, here's your chance, Joycie." They were sponsoring a contest for young, hopeful beauties. We were told to meet on the Ambassador Hotel grounds at an upcoming date. The folks took me there. It was swarming with lovely girls and doting parents. There must have been thousands of girls hoping to be selected for a camera test.

Old-fashioned cameras that you turned with handles were set up everywhere. We were paraded by one at a time as we were called over and asked to turn this way and that, so they could capture our beauty possibilities at various angles. After all, this was the silent days. No voice tests. We left our names and phone number for any future contact.

At the contest, I remember seeing a pretty young girl whom we later learned was Janet Gaynor. Though not chosen as one of the winners for this contest, she was soon discovered and would soon find her way on the path to stardom.

I waited by the phone for any news about the contest. Sure enough, I was called, among many other girls, for the next interview. Not bad, considering the vast numbers who had entered the contest.

My first Hollywood portrait. I'm 17, but look about 12 or 13.

The next phase of the contest was held at First National Studios. I was all dressed up in a little black velvet dress with a stand-up fur collar Mom made for me. Studio executives and talent scouts sat behind a long table. Each girl walked forward, answered a few questions, and made more screen tests. That's it! We left.

The first prize was $500 and a small part in a film. Other winners received a smaller monetary prize.

We watched the paper for the names of the 10 winners. There was little ole Joycie among the names, but a little further down the list. I received $50 for that contest and an invitation to appear at Loew's State Theatre in downtown Los Angeles. When they introduced me, I was instructed to walk across the stage, take my bow, and receive my check.

My folks took me to the theater that night. They were seated in the audience and I was ushered backstage. One by one the girls took their bows and received their checks. When I came out, rather than bowing to the audience, I simply walked across the stage, took my check they handed me, and exited the stage. I totally ignored the audience and forgot to take my bow. The demure little girl from the plains of Oklahoma was mortified.

I knew immediately I had made a big mistake by not taking my bow. After all, isn't that why I was really there, to take my bows, to be seen? I didn't know how to get from backstage to where my parents were sitting, so the next thing I knew, I went out a door and found myself on the street in front of the theater. I was flustered, humiliated, and scared. I couldn't think to go to the ticket window or doorman and tell them I was one of the contest winners and needed to get in to find my parents. Also, I didn't have enough money in my little purse to buy a ticket.

Instead, I got on a streetcar and headed for home. I felt so miserable over my failure of a stage appearance and tried not to cry in front of everyone. I got off a few blocks from home and walked down a very dark Western Avenue. Having no key to get in the house, I went around to the back porch, got in the old swing, and let myself go with tears. I must have cried myself to sleep. So much for the little green kid from Tulsa, I thought.

We found out later that the first prize winner had been a setup. She was a girlfriend of the top man at the newspaper. Such shenanigans were not uncommon in Hollywood, I was to learn.

Soon after this experience, a well-known photographer contacted the winners of the contest and invited us to his studio to take some glamour portraits. After the photo session, he offered to be my manager and agent. He would contact the studios to help secure film roles for me. For his work, he would collect 20 percent of anything I earned. We thought that was okay and I signed. We found out later it was illegal to charge more than 10 percent. In the meantime, however, he had taken lots of great photos, which I would take to casting offices when I applied for work.

Mom had already registered me with an agency that supplied extras to the studios. They paid $7.50 a day and the agency took 10 percent.

The agency kept me quite busy with extra work and Mom stayed occupied on the phones taking calls from studios. The casting offices would tell us the basic instructions. Be dressed for a street, café, or nightclub scene, and be at such and such studio at the appointed time, made up, and ready to work. Yes, in those days, we supplied our own clothes and makeup.

I bought everything Max Factor offered: makeup, powder and puff, plus a little case to carry it all in. I was in the movies, not yet a star, but at least doing some extra work and seeing and learning what moving pictures were all about.

My first job was as one of the hundreds of extras in the candy ball scene in *The Golden Bed* (1925), filmed at the old Famous Players-Lasky Studio on Vine Street in Hollywood. Cecil B. De Mille directed and Rod La Rocque and Lillian Rich were the stars.

I was wide-eyed and in awed wonder at it all. In describing it at home, I said, "Mom, it's just like a big party all day!"

Being in the movies and around those beautiful and glamorous stars was an exciting new world for me. I remember seeing many extras on that film – Charles Farrell was one — who later became movie stars.

I worked on *The Golden Bed* for about three or four weeks and continued doing other extra work. In the process, I got acquainted with casting offices and learned to make my way to the studios.

Part of my education was learning how film schedules worked. For instance, I had a call for a job at Universal Studios, quite a distance from where we lived in Hollywood. Mom and I had to catch multiple streetcars to get there. I was told to come on a certain day. That particular day, it rained. I mean, it poured! So, we decided to wait until a better day. We finally showed up at the studio and announced that I had a casting call. The casting department looked it up and said my call had been several days before. I learned one had to be on time and that no one holds up a studio when a lot of money and other schedules are involved.

As I continued going around to studios with those first portraits tucked under my arm, I began to notice some strange and inquiring looks. Finally, one man said, "If I were you, I wouldn't show those photos around. You look like a nice, innocent kid and showing them will give you a bad reputation. The photographer is a degenerate."

I didn't quite know what a degenerate was. I had heard the word and assumed it was something strange and awful regarding sex. I thanked the man for the warning and decided I'd better leave these photos at home. I told Mom and we talked it over, neither of us could really decide just what a degenerate did.

After that, I never returned to the photographer's studio. I made excuses when he called. He wasn't getting me any work, and I was doing pretty well on my own for the work I was getting.

After months of working as an extra, I heard that First National was plan-

My Mae Murray look.

ning to test some young hopefuls for a long-term studio contract. Those selected would get the buildup to stardom, with worldwide publicity and roles in films with established, older stars, such as Anna Q. Nilsson, Colleen Moore, Corinne Griffith, and Evelyn Brent. Someone got me an appointment and I went over to the studios in Burbank on the appointed date and time. Remember, I aimed never to be late or delay appointments again.

They tested many girls that day. The director told me a few things he wanted me to do. Turn this way and that. I had no reticence whatsoever. With silent films, there were no lines, only looks. I was totally natural and at ease. I did what I was told to do, but I also added whatever I thought would enhance my performance. I decided to do my Mae Murray look. I threw back my head, dropped my eyelids, and gave that bee-stung pucker with my lips.

My Mae Murray look must have done the trick, because the studio called and offered me a contract with yearly options at $100 a week. Before I could get over to Burbank to sign the contract, however, I remembered that management contact I had signed with the degenerate photographer. This man had been haunting me since my first days in Hollywood.

I was in a fix. How could I let the studio know I had this deal? It would probably kill my chances. And, I was sure the photographer could come after me for a commission. How would we keep the photographer from hearing the news of me signing a contract? I could imagine him hanging on and never giving up, causing trouble, suing for a commission, and finally ruining any chances I'd come to Hollywood for in the first place.

Needless to say, we had to act — and act fast! Dad decided to face the photographer and ask for a signed cancellation of the contract on the basis that he'd never gotten me work. The man put up a mean, nasty fight and refused. He was suspicious and wanted to hang on to me. Dad, however, was a good bluffer, too. It was a wild and hectic day.

The photographer demanded that I come in on the scene. I refused to see him. Then, he demanded money for the return of the contract and payment for the photos he'd made. We were stuck, desperate, and poor. Dad finally had to rack up several hundred dollars to pay him off and set me free.

In a few days, I signed with First National and no one at the studio ever knew of our predicament.

Incidentally, he was in a lot of trouble with many Hollywood stars he had photographed and with his shady dealings around town. He was finally run out of the area and his photo business was shut down. One thing is for sure, I bet he was pretty livid when the news came out that I was now under contract to First National.

Hurrah! My career had started. There were photos made at the studio and publicity was generated about my contract. There were pictures of Colleen Moore welcoming me to the studio and one of June Mathis, Al Rockett, and other studio heads watching me sign on the dotted line. It happened rather fast. We had been in Hollywood only three months.

There was hardly a day when I wasn't called to the studio for endless publicity stunts, photo shoots, and personal appearances at every big film or theater opening.

I finally learned how to take a bow on stage, but I was never comfortable being in front of a large group of people. Being before a camera was another matter. I was quite at ease when the cameras rolled. It was like working with a family of other players, all having our lines and scripts to learn.

A 1925 publicity photograph for two of my First National films.

CHAPTER 6 | *I Become a Baby Again, a Baby Again, a Wampas Baby*

Each year, there was a selection by the Western Association of Motion Picture Advertisers (Wampas) of the most promising actresses in Hollywood. It was a huge event, and in those early days, akin to the Academy Awards, which were just a few years away. Not long after I signed with First National, I was named one of the 13 Wampas Baby Stars of 1926.

I was in pretty good company with names like Dolores Costello, Joan Craw-

Edna Marion (right) and I announce the Wampas festivities.

ford, Dolores Del Rio, Fay Wray, Sally Long, Edna Marion, Sally O'Neill, Mary Brian, Mary Astor, Marceline Day, Janet Gaynor, and Vera Reynolds.

Nothing could have put our names on the map as new personalities and candidates for stardom quite like being named a Wampas. There was a big event in Hollywood where we all were introduced to the public and film world. Naturally, this called for a special occasion for each girl to look her best.

So, Mom and I went shopping for that perfect beautiful gown for me. We went to see Bess Schlank, who had one of the top dress designer shops on Hollywood Boulevard. Of course, at $350, the dress we selected was a fortune to us. At today's designer prices, that dress would probably cost several thousand dollars. It was a beauty! White taffeta and layers of white marquisettes as a flounce on the bottom, and handmade flowers of the same material, white pan velvet with silver lame leaves, all beaded in large and small pearls. It was stunning, and I looked pretty elegant wearing it. I felt like I had arrived. If I hadn't arrived, I was at least on the right path.

CHAPTER 7 | An Education in Studio Politics

Being under contract and having been named a Wampas Baby Star, my career was moving along with endless publicity. It got to where I almost — I said, *almost* — hated to hear the phone ring. I was always working in small roles with some of the older and established stars.

In those early days, the studios more or less ran things on the old star system. The story material was written or selected for each of the studio's big stars. The photography in all scenes centered on and catered to them. They had more close-ups and the best lighting. The directors centered their attention on those stars' reaction to any circumstance, more than on the scene being shot.

I began to notice situations which I thought were hindering, not helping, my chances toward success as a film actress. In the early days, it was Corinne Griffith, Colleen Moore, Anna Q. Nilsson, and Evelyn Brent. Later, it was Marlene Dietrich and Alice Faye. They all had major influence about so many things. They liked having their way.

For instance, they would have a say in the casting of certain roles for other actresses who would appear with them in a scene. The studios, too, would make sure there was no competition with their star personalities, whose names carried the picture and influenced the earning capacity at the box office, even if it was a poor production.

I was in a quandary about this at first, being such a newcomer. I hardly realized what was going on, but in some of the last silent pictures, I got more attuned to studio politics.

The director often placed me outside the good lighting. Sometimes, a screen was placed in front of me to make sure that my face and features appeared hazy and to prevent me from appearing younger than the older, established star.

Those practices were especially popular in the silent days when it was your looks that really counted. Then, in the talking films, I still experienced the politics and competitive games that went on. My role was often lessened in a number of ways: photography, lighting, angle shots, and lack of close-ups. Often, a special scene that should have favored me and would have meant so much in featuring my character role, personality, and facial expressions, was lessened or totally lost. A beautiful close-up of the established star would be held to get their reaction to the lines I was spouting off camera. Or, the cameraman would film the scene over my ear or from the back of my head while focusing the shot on the star.

In other words, one becomes the face on the cutting room floor, and one's power to attract or steal a scene is lost in the scuffle for supremacy. Other hindrances were agents who weren't on their toes at the right time or who left town when there could have been a break. Also, another actor's agent could bargain or cut the salary of their client for the studio, or the director might favor a player who could give a lackluster performance, while making sure they wouldn't be any competition to their star.

How often my agent would say, "Honey, I had you up for a great role. You were perfect for the part. The producer or director agreed, but said, 'You know we can't put Joyce opposite so and so. That would be too much competition. She photographs too well or she's a great scene stealer with her cute comedy and special personality. We cannot afford to have our star's popularity in jeopardy. There's too much money involved.'"

I often said, "Mom, I don't know how I even get a job with all one has to deal with."

While under contract to Fox, the studio brought Una Merkel from the Broadway stage and gave her all the good comedy and Southern roles that were my stock and trade, while I was pushed into other roles that were not my type.

Also, after making several films with Janet Gaynor at Fox, I was getting such good reviews against her more mousey-type roles, she put her foot down, having some clout with the studio head Winnie Sheehan, and knocked me out of roles in her films.

One other thing the moviegoing public may not know involves how meager the salaries could be. I could have a seemingly great part that runs off and on through the whole production and seem like a whole month's worth of work. But, the director might schedule my role to be filmed in one, two, or three days and concentrate on my scenes only. That role, in my day, might have paid $100 or $200 a day. After deductions (taxes, agents, for example), I might get only half the gross. Yet, it would have appeared that I worked during the whole production.

CHAPTER 8 | A Romance at First National

After securing the contract at First National, we moved from the small duplex on North Hobart to a one-bedroom apartment in a four-unit building. It was surely nothing fancy, but it was close to the studio, so I could walk over when they called me to work.

After I got settled at the studio, Dad got restless again. He'd hardly been able to bring in a dime. We only had my little contract earnings to live on for rent, utilities, food, clothing, and the other necessities for the three of us. He decided Mom and I would be okay without him. He still had that burning passion to try his luck in Florida. What did he do? He headed east for the Sunshine State.

Mom and I were alone and on our own again, taking streetcars or footing it. Occasionally, she would round up a neighbor or some friend to drive me to the studio. What a luxury to be able to avoid crowded streetcars.

During my time at First National, I attracted an ardent admirer. He was head of props and set design, in charge of all things that furnished and made the set ready for photographing scenes for a film. He had a lot of responsibility.

Darrell started at First National as a teenager sweeping sets and doing odd jobs, until his boss, Thomas Little, moved on to another studio. Darrell stepped into his shoes and took that job.

He was a very fine, dedicated, and responsible young man in his twenties. He and his family, which consisted of his parents and three brothers, had emigrated from Jamaica.

Darrell was a blessing and a great protection for me at an innocent time in my life. He was someone decent to date and was often able to run over with his car and drive me to the studio for my many appointments. He took good care of me and had great respect for Mom. He was also loyal and loving to his parents.

Along the way, however, he became seriously enamored of me to the point of being extremely jealous and possessive. He followed on my heels when I was at the studio. If I was in a photography session at the studio, he would show up to check on my every move. If he saw me walking arm in arm with someone on the lot, he commented with jealousy. Needless to say, his behavior became bothersome. I was too young and busy starting a career for such seriousness.

With Dad gone and Mom and I alone, we just went along with it all. Darrell was such a help. He told Mom he wanted to marry me. She discouraged the idea, telling him that I wasn't in love with him and that marriage surely wasn't on my mind. I didn't have the capacity to care deeply for anyone at this point.

I started secretly dating a handsome fellow I'd met on some picture I was on. If I couldn't see Darrell for the evening, he would come by late at night and slide a box of candy, roses, and a love note on the front porch. Mom would go out and bring them in to me. She and I would sit up like two girls at a slumber party. We'd read the letter, eat the candy, and smell the roses. We had fun being girls together.

This went on awhile, until one evening, the fellow I was dating stayed in the doorway for a goodnight kiss. Darrell, checking up on me, drove by, saw my date, and followed him as he left. The next day, Darrell faced me with his anger and said he had seen the fellow at the studio. I had to make a decision. I wasn't engaged, of course, just had sort of a steady date. I realized Darrell was of more value than the passing fancy, so I quit my double life.

Before I realized it, a year had gone by and it was option time at First National. Without much warning, I was released from my contract and sent to the street, so to speak. We were stunned. How could this be? We thought a five- or seven-year contract meant just that! I hadn't thought about what contract options really meant, that a studio could say goodbye and good luck. I was flabbergasted.

No more steady income for Joyce. I was thrown back into cold, cruel, competitive Hollywood. The studio heads assured me I was young yet — at 19 — and that I'd be okay. I could easily find other work in the movies.

Dad had been writing that the boom in Florida was at the tail end by the time he arrived in Florida. The bottom had dropped out of the real estate business and he had no money. His last sentence read something like, "Hang on to every dollar you have. I'm coming home — broke!"

So, Dad rejoined us, barely making it back to Hollywood in whatever car he had been able to get while there.

We all seemed to be starting over, taking our chances in whatever life had ahead for us. At least I had some experience and was somewhat of a known name, thanks to all the worldwide publicity the studio had given me.

I had a big scrapbook full of lovely photos and publicity write-ups. Fan mail was coming in. So, it wasn't too difficult for me to find an agent to represent me and keep me alive at the studios. I embarked on my freelance career.

CHAPTER 9 | The Freedom of Freelancing

We finally got out of the financial hole we were in and, with a few dollars, decided we could make a down payment on a little house on Edenhurst Avenue, near Glendale. It was five rooms for $500 down and $50 a month. Dad stayed around more to help us and to drive me to the studios for interviews and film shoots.

There soon came the rumbles of an economic depression and stock market

One of my favorite wall hangings, 1929.

trouble. Tension and strife was on for everyone. Soon, Dad had to leave and seek some source of earnings. He tried sales and commission in new areas. We told him if he could keep himself up and send us $50 a month for the house payment, we would try to make out for groceries and our necessities.

In the late 1920s, following my First National contact, I began freelancing. While continuing in films, Mom and I met some people in the business of dog and cat breeding. We thought this might be something we could do at home while I waited for studio calls.

I also discovered that I had some art talent, and while being home bound and waiting for the phone to ring, I did some pretty good oil paintings. Also, using monks cloth and thinned-down oils, I painted some wall hangings.

While I didn't find a way of selling much, I traded one of my tapestries and bought a thoroughbred Belgian Griffon. I swapped another piece of art for its breeding. I joined the American Kennel Club so that I could get my papers and put the dogs in shows.

Mingling with animal lovers was a new world for me. They were a strange group in many ways. But, we made some great pets as friends and had us a wee business — we thought!

We even sent Dad some of my art and he traded it for room and board at some boarding house. We were all struggling on with life's difficulties.

The animals turned out to be a lot of care and cost. Keeping them free of fleas, bathed, healthy, and fed was a major chore. I became a pretty good vet and pet doctor. The Griffons had their tails bobbed a few days after birth. I did those procedures with one of Dad's sterilized razors. Putting the tiny tail on the bread board in the kitchen, I sliced away. One squeal and it was over. Mom would run out of the house in horror every time I performed my amputations.

There were ads to run for breedings or dog sales. Often, we could sell a baby for only $10, not a lot of money when we considered how much went into them. Then, there was a yearly tax for each dog.

A lot of work went into taking care of these dogs and we found not much, if any, gain. Then came my introduction to the new medium that was destined to change the motion picture industry — talkies! My career took off.

CHAPTER 10 | *Clara and I Break into the Talkies*

I continued raising and selling puppies between film roles in the last years of the silent era. I did two comedies with Madge Bellamy at Fox and my first Western at Universal. They were not great roles for me, but at least I was working. In 1929, with the advent of sound, my career gained momentum with the exciting offer that came from Paramount to appear with the big brown-eyed and beautiful Clara Bow.

The Wild Party was particularly memorable because it provided our debut into the new medium of talking pictures. In The Wild Party, I played a little snoop, always telling tales on my girlfriends in the dormitory and butting in on everyone's business. This, of course, endeared me to my dorm mates. It was great characterization and perhaps the best film role I'd had thus far. The director, Dorothy Arzner, was so complimentary of my work and what I had put into the part. I am sure she gave me a boost with the studio heads.

We barely finished The Wild Party before I was cast again with Clara in Dangerous Curves, a circus story set under the big top.

Clara and I were bareback riders on big dappled-gray horses. We were put into harnesses that lifted and swung us into position as the horse galloped by. Our costumes were black tights and little ruffled tutus. Clara had a rounded figure, while I was quite slender. While she looked perfectly gorgeous in the costume, I thought I looked like a black widow spider.

The two Bow pictures were filmed part silent and part sound. The studios were not yet equipped with soundproof stages, so we shot the films at night when traffic and outside sounds were minimal. When I say we shot at night, I mean, all night! A studio car would pick me up early every evening and bring me home the next morning.

While I adored Clara, the two films we did together were hard work! They were long hours without any union protection for our health, proper rest, and overtime pay.

I took my favorite Griffon puppy, Muggins, to the studio. She was a lot of company during the long night hours. When we weren't in scenes or needed on the set immediately, we could leave the warmth of the salamanders and go to rest in our dressing rooms until the assistant called us to the set.

While much has been written about Clara's fear of the microphone, she seemed to me to be perfectly at ease. A great demand was placed on her shoulders, as her name carried the picture.

At midnight, lunch was called, and we dined in the commissary. I would get a steak or something that I could share with Muggins in our room.

Between scenes, professional musicians played a portable piano and violin to keep the mood until the next scene.

I adored Clara. What a trouper! She was so strong and full of vitality. Even in the middle of the night, after having worked for hours, she was bright-eyed and bushy-tailed. Usually, she had her eye on some young fellow, be it an actor or electrician, whoever interested her. Then, off to her dressing room they'd go when time allowed or when work was over. Clara was always intertwined with romance.

Later in Clara's career, scandalmongers brought out cruel and vicious reports about her. They were passing out handbills around the studio and outside on the

Clara Bow (left) and I in our circus costumes from Dangerous Curves.

streets. By them hawking their filth, I'm sure it crushed this poor girl and her career. It wasn't fair. She was very sweet, just tempted and driven, I suppose.

I credit Rex Bell, with whom I worked in *Lightnin'*, with rescuing Clara. They married and he tried to straighten her out through his Christian Science beliefs.

About the time I worked with Clara Bow.

CHAPTER 11 | *Salute!*

On the merits of my performances in the two Bow films, Paramount came to me with a contract offer. I'd learned at First National that signing things was not always to my advantage. I detested the tricks usually buried in contracts. This particular one was a poor financial offer with six-month options. I had experience with options and decided not to sign.

Dying my hair red gave me a whole new image for the screen.

Besides, as I was finishing *Dangerous Curves* at Paramount, I got a nice role in Salute, a Fox film that was going into production right away. I would be traveling on location to Annapolis, Maryland, with a fantastic cast that included George O'Brien and Helen Chandler. The great John Ford was directing.

I was thrilled about the role, of course, but *Salute* came on the tails of the two

Helen Chandler, William Janney, and I stand behind George O'Brien on the set of Salute. COURTESY OF WILLIAM JANNEY.

Bow films, which were unusually hard shoots that involved all-night work. I was physically worn down and not prepared to leave home for a strenuous film shoot.

Being physically weak from childhood, I knew I needed all the rest and care I could get. So, I was able to talk the studio into paying Mom's way to chaperone and take care of me on the long trip east.

I dyed my hair red after the Bow pictures thinking it might change my image from an innocent ingénue to a more seductive something or other. It worked! I found out when the academy boys and others on location began hanging around and asking me out.

Was I ever glad I asked Mom to come along with me, because the action started before we pulled out of the Santa Fe station in Los Angeles. The whole University of Southern California football team was with us, including John Wayne and Ward Bond, both of whom had played for the team. While we had a wait in Chicago, the guys took off and disappeared. When it was time to board the train for our trip to Maryland, many were missing. Those in charge wrung their hands and looked everywhere for the stragglers.

When they finally showed up, the stories they told about their adventures were entertaining and scandalous. Drinking, wild women, the works! Ward Bond was particularly fond of Mom and would sit by her and roll his head on her bosom and tell her everything that went on. Even John Ford, or "Pappy," as we called him, had plenty to tell.

A young girl from the New York stage, Helen Chandler, had the other female role in the picture. One could never meet a more sweet and innocent-appearing person. But, there was another side to Helen that raised plenty of eyebrows. Let's put it like this, she could really put away a tumbler of gin.

The cast was housed at the beautiful Carvel Hall in Annapolis. It had such atmosphere. In fact, the whole town did, with quaint streets laid with brick. Mom and I shared a room. I was surely glad she was with me; otherwise, I would have had to share a room with the unpredictable Helen and all her goings on. It would have been a nightmare for me.

Pappy Ford, whose nickname for me was "Chinkapin," seemed to like me and tried to protect me from the wild stuff. I was very still very childlike for my age, probably, I suspect, from being from such a sheltered family. It was also part of my nature. I wasn't a rebellious type, nor was I pawing the air to jump into the things of the world.

Pappy recognized my innocence and came to my defense. At some dinner party in Annapolis, I was seated next to him. I was toying with a rose at my plate and not having much to say. One of the men remarked that I was unsophisticated. Pappy spoke up and defended me saying, "Leave her alone. She's young yet."

As a rule, I was never interested in actors and seldom dated them. They seemed to be all ego and narcissism. Most of the guys I dated were not part of the film industry. I admit, however, that I did have a thing for George O'Brien. He seemingly didn't return the interest. He was just a polite gentleman. There was no sparkle or flirtation. I guess I wasn't his type, or he may have been taken up elsewhere, for he later married the actress Marguerite Churchill. He was very careful of me and was a solid man of standards and principles.

A rather amusing thing happened at a party during the filming of *Salute*. I had been dancing with George. We sat down to rest. I noticed him looking at me. Finally, he leaned over and said quietly, "Honey, fix your dress." I looked down and a saw a little bosom padding had crept up and was showing above my black velvet evening dress. I quickly shoved it back in place. Ah, my rosy cheeks of embarrassment!

George O'Brien and Joel McCrea, with whom I later appeared in *Lightnin'*, were the only actors I knew that I felt were sweet men of high quality.

CHAPTER 12 | *Joycie, Janet, and Joel at Fox*

I had recently turned down a deal to work with Paramount because the deal didn't feel right to me. After my work in *Salute* was complete and I was back in Hollywood, I began to contemplate a deal with Fox. I seemed well liked by the studio executives and my work in *Salute* was okay, I thought. I didn't have an agent working on my behalf at that time, so I decided to approach some of the Fox Studio heads on my own. I told them I'd had an offer from Paramount, but that after working in *Salute*, I preferred working at Fox. Would they be interested in me? They talked it over and said they would. I named my price — a bit above Paramount's offer — and asked for a yearly option. The studio agreed to my offer and I was happily on a payroll once more. I was secure for 12 months, at least.

After signing with Fox, I splurged a bit and bought a $500 baby grand piano and my first fur coat. While Mom and I were walking down Hollywood Boulevard one afternoon, I saw a lady with a fur jacket that really caught my eye. I hurried alongside her and inquired about it. She said it was Russian Fitch, beautiful cream-colored fur with gold and brown markings. I went shopping and found what I wanted.

It was a hardy fur and I wore it to the studio, on location, and to film premieres. It still hangs in my closet with a few other furs I acquired along the way. It's rather worn, but is still a good skin. I hate to part with it. I often throw it over my bed like a robe on a cold night.

At Fox, I got some great publicity and they seemed to be planning a big buildup of my career. I was busier than I'd ever been. Dad was on hand to drive me to the studio and to various social activities. I didn't have the time and attention to care for all the animals we had acquired, so I sold them off to other breeders and pet show people. I kept four of my favorites: Muggins, the Griffon; her son, a toy Pekinese; and one silver Persian cat, Gloria.

I also settled my ongoing relationship with Darrell. Not really knowing or being experienced or sophisticated in breakups, I handled it so badly and somewhat cruelly. All I could think of that would really make it final was to tell him I was in love with someone else. That someone else was George O'Brien. I told him I had fallen for him during our trip to Annapolis. Poor Darrell gave up, saying, "I can't begin to compete with George O'Brien."

What a heartbreak I'd given. Darrell got ulcers over his grief. His family was also very hurt and stopped speaking to me. He'd been around for three years, but I finally realized I couldn't let him go on dangling and hoping for something more. I realize now that I could have been more gentle and explanatory of how I didn't care as much as he did.

I was free now, so to speak, and in love with love after that. I had little flirtations and infatuations, but I never really found another loyal and loving heart in a man that cared so deeply. Some years later, I heard his beloved mother had died and I wrote a condolence note. He came to see me and I could tell he still

Modeling my Russian Fitch fur.

cared and would have easily fallen into the tender trap again. I had no encouragement to offer. Later, he found and married a divorced lady with a daughter. They had a child of their own, which thrilled him. They had a good life, traveled, and owned a nice home. He's been successful. My life continued in another pattern of events.

Fox cast me in some pretty good roles, such as *High Society Blues* with Janet

Hedda Hopper, Janet Gaynor, me, and Charles Farrell in High Society Blues.

Gaynor and Charles Farrell. The little girl (Gaynor) I'd seen way back in the contest we were in was now a star. Hedda Hopper, not yet the gossip queen she became, and that dear Louise Fazenda, were also in the cast.

The Three Sisters was a good dramatic role for me. I was one of three sisters, the others being June Collyer and Addie McPhail. Our Italian mother was Louise Dresser.

In the film, I stab the village baker on the night of my wedding. I escape and eventually come to prosperity in the United States. I liked the film because I got to play a fiery girl and dance the Tarantella.

While I was at the studio, Janet Gaynor started having trouble with Winnie Sheehan over money, I believe. She left the studio awhile and Fox decided they would team me with Charles Farrell. The publicity department made many pictures of us together as a romantic twosome. Gaynor heard about it and hurried back to recap her position. So, nothing came of those plans. Her roles were rather a mousey type and whenever we had parts in the same film, my comedy stuff began to overshadow her personality. I got outstanding reviews from the exhibitors and the public. So, what did Janet do? She used her sway with Sheehan to cut me out of appearing in her pictures.

I kept busy in other films and didn't worry too much about Janet Gaynor. I was cast as Diana in *Lightnin'* and sent on location to Lake Tahoe with Joel McCrea and Will Rogers, both of whom I liked very much. The plot, as I recall,

Fox had ideas about teaming me with Charles Farrell.

had to do with divorce and the problems couples have in meeting the residency requirements for getting a divorce in Nevada.

Lake Tahoe was the perfect location for a film shoot and we were housed in the rustic Tahoe Tavern and taken to the location site every morning for work. I believe we also had sets there that we used for interiors.

Rex Bell was my husband in the picture and Will Rogers gave us his famous wisdom and tried to get us back together. It was during this time that Rex was involved with Clara Bow and she stayed at the Cal-Neva hotel to be near. They married not long after.

Being on location with *Lightnin'* was one of my favorite film experiences. Every day at noon, the chow truck came from the commissary with an abundance of good food. Long tables and benches were set up under the pines by the lake where the cast and crew gathered to eat. Between scenes and back at the lodge in the evenings, there was time to visit and get acquainted with other cast members.

Joel McCrea and I found we liked each other right away and there was a drifting together. We had similar values, standards, and interests. We were also spiritually compatible, although he was into Christian Science and I came from a Methodist, Presbyterian, and Baptist background.

After dinner every evening, we walked the moonlit paths around the lake and tavern grounds. We did a lot of talking, walking, and holding hands. Soon came the inevitable sweet, tender kissing. Joel was not overpowering; there was just a mutual feeling beginning to develop between us.

We talked about Hollywood and some of the temptations that comes with the territory. He told me of some big female stars who had gone after him and tried to work him over and seduce him. His values and strength of character, he said, held things in check, much to the frustration of the older actresses.

Joel said he had other goals in life besides films and acting. He would use this medium to get his start, then buy land and become a rancher.

Will Rogers called me "Red," because I kept my hair that color while at Fox. The attraction Joel and I had for each other didn't get past this wise man. He began to butt in and would warn Joel, "Be careful of Red," which I didn't appreciate. He was really trying to influence Joel against me, which I thought was rather mean.

Along the way, Joel said, "After I get that ranch, you might just be out there on it with me." That sounded good to a girl who loved that kind of simple, rustic life.

Some of us finished our scenes and were sent home. Joel heard I was leaving and came to tell me goodbye. He really showed how much he would miss me! He also sent a telegram saying so when I returned.

We were both just at the start of our careers and our work kept us busy and pulling in opposite directions. He came to see me a couple of times in Hollywood. Later he met actress Frances Dee on a film (*The Silver Cord*, I believe). The die was cast; they fell in love and married. Frances got to live on the ranch. So goes fate!

Many years later, I was dating someone who also knew Joel. We were out driving in the area of Joel's ranch and he suggested we drive back and visit Joel and Frances. When I saw him this time, he was just an old cowhand, nothing of the Joel I'd known for a short time. But, I wondered for a moment, what it would have been like if I'd been on his ranch all this time.

CHAPTER 13 | *Living the Hollywood Life*

I'd been at Fox for a while and with all the publicity I was getting and films I was doing, we decided we should put ourselves into a better background than the small house we had bought in Glendale. Looking in Beverly Hills behind the Beverly Hills Hotel, we found an area called Beverly Glen. Its winding roads go through the hills clear to the Valley area where I now live.

This stunning house sat back from the street and up a sloped hill with wind-

I really felt like a movie star when we moved to Beverly Glen.

ing stone steps that reached the front door.

A private road ran back of the house where the garage and servants' quarters sat. It was so beautiful with its manicured landscape and abundance of flowers. It really looked like a house where an actress should be living. The owners were a famous dance team, husband and wife, who were on the road most of the time.

I loved the atmosphere and décor of the house. My bedroom wall was detailed with hand-painted clusters of lavender wisteria. The rather modern furnishings were lavender and silver trim. French doors opened onto a little balcony overlooking the flowered terrace and stone work that sloped down to the street. The living room had a huge wine-colored velvet sofa that ran along the length of the wall beneath paneled mirrors. With its abundance of pillows to melt into, I called it my "sex appeal couch."

With the Depression just getting under way, we leased this furnished house for a song. Living expenses were cheap, and with my steady income from Fox, we had never had it this good. Also, Dad was around during this time and helped me get to and from the studio.

Things were going so well that we also got a big, beautiful car now and then. Dad and I would go shopping in Beverly Hills where moneyed people were turning in cars for new ones every three or four years. So, we often found a luxury Lincoln or Cadillac for around $2,000 cash. This was the joy of the Depression,

Reclining on my sex appeal sofa

if one had a few dollars coming in.

We rented our little bungalow in Glendale and moved my baby grand piano, along with my three dogs and cat, to Beverly Glen.

The studio sent photographers out from time to time to take photos of me for magazines and interviews.

We, in time, got some live-in help for the area out back. The city was full of young fellows needing a free home, food, and small pay. They were just happy to have a place off the streets. We even had parents who would bring their sons and ask us to keep them, because they couldn't, and there was no work.

We fixed these guys up with a chauffeur's coat and cap for driving me around and a serving coat for serving food and drink when we had dinner parties. Our helpers kept the house clean so that Mom could rest for the first time in her life. Mom, however, continued doing her own fabulous cooking. Being up in the canyon, we had to shop for our food in Beverly Hills, where prices were higher than in Hollywood or Glendale.

I'd take nice walks with my pups through the canyon and around the neighborhood. I found that Jean Harlow lived on one of the side streets when she had that strange marriage to Paul Bern. We would see them pass by on their way in and out. We were living there when their trouble happened and the scandal broke of their unusual relationship, her unhappiness, and his alleged suicide.

A self portrait I did in charcoal.

Just above us high in the hills on Bella Drive was Falcon Lair, the former estate of Rudolph Valentino. Winnie Sheehan, the head of Fox Studios, had a gorgeous mansion nearby, where he hosted many fabulous parties.

At the entrance of Beverly Glen was Harold Lloyd's massive estate, a mansion and acres of landscaped grounds. We passed the estate every time we came or went from our home. Massive gates at the entrance were usually kept open so anyone passing could see a big fish pond in a lush garden a little ways past the entrance.

We also had a small fish pond in our yard. A mob of big, fat frogs made their abiding place in our little pond. At night, they croaked and made such a noise that none of the Comptons could sleep.

I had a bright idea. I got a large gunny sack and stick, and with Dad's help, the two of us prodded those frogs into the bag. As we drove by Lloyd's estate one evening, Dad stopped and dumped those little toads at the gate and shooed them towards the pond. They went hopping happily towards their new home. Two good things came out of our adventure: we were able to sleep at night and the frogs found a good home.

I didn't have time or any particular interest in seeking personal friendships with the many film people with whom I worked. Most of us were too busy with our careers, families, and friends outside of the industry. I was more interested in my own personal hobbies apart from my work. It was good to get away from the whole aspect of acting and studio activity between films.

For example, I was into my painting and art work, and I'd also taken up designing and making my personal wardrobe. I never used patterns. My designs were completely original. Mom also made her own wardrobe. We would help each other with the fittings and everything that was involved in putting the material together.

We shopped in downtown Los Angeles several times a year. Dad would drive us to all the major department stores to find our beautiful materials for our sewing. Mom and I would buy reams and reams of interesting yardage to work with all year. I kept Mom looking like a grand dame. All fixed up, she was handsome lady. We saved on our outfits and splurged on expensive hats and fur coats, when summer sales were on. One time, I bought three furs in one shopping spree.

With my collection of furs and fancy dresses, I really looked like a picture actress when I went to interview for a role. We really dressed in those days: hats, bags, gloves, beautiful shoes, the whole ensemble. I often created my own hats and bags out of the same fabric as the dress.

People would say, "That girl must spend a fortune on her clothes." My dates thought so, too, when they took me dancing to nice hotels and nightclubs.

As a contract player at Fox, I was expected to participate in some of the Hollywood social life. There were grand parties with big stars, all for the purpose of being seen and publicized in the film news. I did it all in my time.

I remember one particular party at Winnie Sheehan's estate. I was a guest among many, including the beautiful Gloria Swanson and Constance Bennett. Humphrey Bogart was also among the guests. I had met and danced with Bogey. Afterwards, we wandered into the lovely, moonlit garden to get the evening breeze. Some bits of conversation ensued and he remarked how beautiful I looked in the moonlight. In some way, we sort of gravitated together and had some nice smooching. It just seemed like the thing to do.

Louella Parsons had news items the next day commenting on what the stars were wearing. Louella went on to write, "Joyce Compton took the cake in a stunning creation from Paris!" Mom and I got a giggle over that one. For we, Mom and I, not Paris, had gotten me together. I got a strip of black velvet and wound it around my 110 pounds. One end went over one shoulder, leaving the other bare.

I instructed Mom, "Pin here, tuck there." Then, we'd sew a strand of white gardenias across the back strip of velvet crossing my back from one shoulder to the waist. It was simple, but very effective. I had Mom sew me in it, so nothing would come apart. She had to get the scissors to "unzip" me when I got home. I wouldn't wear a stitch underneath when I dressed for a night out like this. I didn't need or own a girdle, nor did I want a panty line to show! Of course, she wanted to hear all about the party, who was there, that sort of thing.

At another big affair later on, I came up with something original to compete with my former design success. It was somewhat of a copy of the black velvet creation, only in the sexiness of a clinging silver lame, with two large wine-colored velvet roses, one at the shoulder, the other at the hip. One of the directors I had worked with wandered over with a drink in his hand and exclaimed, "I could just rip that dress right off you." What better compliment?

When I wasn't busy on a picture, there were always things to do. I went often to the studio for magazine or newspaper interviews and to the portrait gallery for endless photography sessions. I'd frequent the studio commissary for lunch where I could see and be seen. I'd sit down and chat with directors or pop in some producer's office to see what was in the works. Before I'd leave, I would stroll down to the publicity department, where I would go through the photo stills made on sets while shooting a film and order a set for me or whomever I might have as an agent. I'd finally drop in the mail department and pick up the fan mail.

I got fan mail both at the studios and at home when fans learned of my address. The studios took care of some of my mail and Mom did her share. Dad had to see some young fellows who would show up and send them on their way. (He'd say, "Go home, boys. Joyce can't give you a job.") I began to be recognized on the street and was often hounded while trying to shop. My parents always went with me for protection. This part was annoying, especially when they just pushed themselves in my face.

When I was getting established in films, Mom and Dad had to run from all kinfolks from Kentucky who wanted to come to California and move in with us. They would write and ask for help. I even had a request once from a distant relative asking me to help them bury their dead.

When I was not working at the studio, there was usually sewing going on. If I was too busy, we had a lady seamstress, Miss Stole, who came and lived with us

In off white agora.

a couple of weeks. One winter, I dressed in all white or off-white wallens angora. It was quite stunning and flattering with my red hair. For evening gowns, I wore white pan velvet and chartreuse.

Dating and social events filled in what other time I had, and here and there, I was loaned out to other studios for a film or two.

For some of the big events, Howard Sheehan, studio executive and brother of Winnie, always seemed to turn up to nail me as the lady of his choice to hang on his arm and show off for the evening. Howard was older than me and a bit short and pudgy. He was head of the West Coast theaters, I believe. He liked for me and the other girls working at Fox to accompany him. Howard and I had many mutual friends, such as Jack Gardner, casting executive for Fox, and his lovely wife, Louise Dresser.

Howard was a great friend and decent escort. He was cute and fun and he enjoyed me and my sense of humor.

At one of his many penthouse dinner parties, he popped in with the comment that he thought "having an affair with me would be so spectacular, it would make a fellow's hat stand up on his head."

I came back with the typical Joycie comment, "Why, Howie, would you wear a hat?"

CHAPTER 14 | *We Lose it All*

I often talked with Howard Sheehan about investments and had asked his opinion about putting some of my little savings from my Fox income into the Bank of Hollywood, at the corner of Hollywood and Vine. He had inside information on many business ventures. He said that strategy was okay, but advised, "Don't put it all in one place. Look around and see what others offer."

This bank gave us six percent compound interest and we could draw out as needed without penalty. I told my folks what Howard advised. We went to other banking institutions to see what was available. Other banks seemed more complicated than our institution, so we let it slide and took no action.

One evening, Howard asked if we had divided our account and put some money in other banks. I said we had looked, but had made no change. He said there was going to be some trouble at the Bank of Hollywood and urged me to go the next day to see if we could draw out any money.

The next day, on a chilly December morning in 1930, we took the bank book and went to make a withdrawal. No one could get a dime. By the next morning, the big news was out — the bank had failed!

Elderly people were sitting on the curb and standing around the bank weeping and holding their useless bank books. Their lifesavings were gone.

Many of filmdom's elite, such as John Barrymore, Wallace Beery, and Harry Langdon, were among those I heard who lost everything.

I heard a fantastic story of how Jack Oakie's mother saved his fortune in this bank closure. Shortly before it happened, she had an instinct or premonition to go to the bank and draw out all of Jack's money. The bank told her they didn't have that much money on hand. She said they would wait until they got it from other banks. Finally, it was all together. They put the money into paper bags and newspapers and walked out with Jack's lifesavings. Many years later in Jack's home, I brought up the story to him and his wife, Vicky, and he said, "Was so!"[1]

I tried to comfort Mom about the loss. I had six months at Fox before another option came up and we still had our small home in Glendale. We wouldn't exactly be on the streets. However, Mom's grief was deep. I thought she would never lift her spirits. It really put a pall over things for a while.

Over the next few months, my perspective on life shifted. I often came home weeping from the glamorous social events. "What in the world is the matter with you?" I asked myself. Why this empty feeling? Didn't I have what most young girls longed for, a movie career, the attention, a measure of success? Why was it all becoming so much tinsel? People seemed shallow and self-centered and egos had center stage in their lives.

Even the film roles I often played seemed so foolish and silly, and I would think, "What a way to make a living." But, I didn't know any other profession. It

[1] Jack Oakie writes about the event in *Jack Oakie's Double Takes*, Strawberry Hill Press, 1980.

had all been Mom's idea, a dream of security for me and, I imagine, some dream ambitions of her own lived out through me. Perhaps her feelings of insecurity came because of Dad's up and down business ventures. I went along with her ideas as things developed, not knowing or even thinking of any difference. But, in the last months of my Fox contract, I found my heart wasn't really in my work. I found I wasn't driven by ambition.

Working in films became hard, grueling work with long and tedious hours. As talkies began to take hold, I would work all day and often into the night. It took a toll on my strength and I was often dragging and pushing myself through it all, with the realization that I had to support us all and that there was no other way.

Mom worried about me and worked to keep me on my feet and ready for those work calls. She was always writing to these faith ministries to pray that I would continue to get work and that her frail little girl would get through the job. It seemed to work. I made it and I'm still here!

Mom and I always had a strong faith. She was a pretty good Bible student from her youth. After the bank failure wiped out our savings, she talked it over with me. She said that we had left God out of our finances. I drew closer to my faith during these dark days. I saw why I had wept and felt my emptiness. It was the Holy Spirit drawing me closer. I began to pull away from the social side of my career and just take the film work as I would any other job I might do, as if I were pounding a typewriter.

CHAPTER 15 | *Out Foxed*

After the bank failure, we had to make plans and figure our next move. Dad decided he needed to leave us and see what he could find to do elsewhere. We were left to carry on with the help of a live-in driver to help us get around.

In the meantime, Fox Studios was making some changes and planning to leave the old Western Avenue lot to build a new studio, Fox Hills, out in Westwood. Their new studio would be better equipped for talking pictures.

There were also rumors of a housecleaning of their stock contract people. It was inevitable that I would be caught up in this shakeup and clear that option time would be another blow to us. When a studio has plans to drop you, their attention goes with it. They treat you with little dignity. They practically use you for bit parts or extra work, where originally, they had plans and promises for stardom. They can do this because you are on their payroll. If you refuse, they can dump you and save on the remainder of your contract. I could not afford this price for my feelings or dignity. So, I stuck it out to my last dollar's pay. Then, I was on my own, once again, a freelancer.

Knowing what was coming, Mom gave the renters notice they had to move from our house in Glendale. We then sent our help over to clean up a bit. Soon, we were packed up and back where we started.

The little house was somewhat rundown by now. The Depression was still on, so living and help were cheap. We hired a young man as a driver and for general help around the house. We fixed him up with living quarters in the garage.

We got some work done on the house. A fellow in need helped us pull off old bulging wallpaper and whitewash the walls. We painted the outside white after some dingy color, put up some brown wooden shutters on either side of the windows, and with touches here and there, it wasn't so bad. We still had a home for the price of our mortgage, $50 a month. I did all the mowing, making flowers beds, and general yard work.

The fellow we hired was a small man named Caesar, so we called him Little Caesar. Sometimes things didn't run too smoothly with him. Mom was boss and gave the directions. Often, there were attitudes flying both ways. Little Caesar liked driving me around and the activity that went along with it, rather than helping Mom in the kitchen and house.

We decided we needed to ask Dad to come home and help us, since it was just Mom and me. The day Dad returned, Mom and I had gone shopping with Little Caesar. He had weekends off and was hurrying us home so he could leave. He began driving very erratically and barely missed approaching cars. Mom called out to him sharply, "What do you think you're doing?" He began mumbling back at her reprimand. Mom's Southern blood began to steam, and she snapped. "Shut up," she said. I began to poke Mom because I could sense the danger and hostility coming from Little Caesar.

My Fox look.

When we got to our house, his anger was in full gear. He was raging. As he darted into the driveway, he mowed down a hedge. Mom started screaming. Caesar put the car in reverse and stepped on the gas full force and shot the backwards across the street and into a house. The lady living there had just seconds to move from in front of a picture window where she had been sitting.

One could tell from the whole procedure that Caesar had gone off his rocker in rage and was in a frenzy to do us harm. When the car hit, the motor stopped and he frantically tried to start it up. I felt that if he did, he would have taken off and mowed down anything or anyone in front of him.

By that time, the neighbors had called the police. When I knew Mom was safe, I dashed across the street to get Dad. When the police arrived, I explained the situation and they took Caesar in for questioning. Of course, he denied any intent to harm us and said he had lost control of the car. An ambulance came and took Mom to the emergency room. She was quite shaken up. I went with her in the ambulance; Dad followed in our car. There was no physical damage to Mom: nothing was broken, only our shattered nerves.

We had to repair the damage to the house next door, as we had no insurance. They could have sued, but didn't. The police got in touch and wanted to know whether we wanted to press charges. We didn't think it would do any good, as we couldn't prove anything about his intent to harm us.

Mom continued in an awful state of collapse. She spent a lot of time in bed, shaking from head to toe with nerves. In the middle of all that, I got a picture job. I would work all day, then come home and hold her in bed during the night. We decided we were not able to go through some useless court procedure or try to prove anything. We considered ourselves lucky and hoped we never saw Caesar again.

One day, a week later, Mom was lying on the couch in the living room. We looked up and saw Caesar looking in through the screen door. Mom called for Dad and nearly passed out at the sight of the fellow.

By the time Dad got the full impact of the story and the intent of the accident, his Southern blood was in high boil. We saw Caesar had brought a whole carload of friends with him and we feared Dad would stir up more trouble. Caesar, it turned out, had only come to pick up some of his possessions.

Our Caesar nightmare ended without incident.

CHAPTER 16 | *New York, New York*

With very little happening in my career or at home, I decided to take a train trip to New York — just me! The train ride across the country took four hot and muggy days in June.

I had quite a few friends in New York, among them an executive I'd known at Fox, Joe Johnson, his wife, and daughter. They had an apartment on 5th Avenue. I wired them of my intent and that I would probably stay a few months and investigate the possibilities of film work on the East Coast.

A former agent tried to coax me to go, saying, "Joycie, you would be just perfect on the stage. Audiences would love you. Then, Hollywood would call you back and it would give your career a big boost."

I, however, had great insecurity about appearing before a live audience. Even taking a bow, as you remember, was enough to make me absentminded. So, appearing on the stage didn't appeal to me.

I had also kept a diary through some of my Hollywood years and intended to put together a book. I saw a lot of fun and interesting story material. I wrote on the train and in between activities in New York.

I let the Johnsons know when my train would arrive. They had a room held for me at The Warwick, then a very nice hotel. They agreed to meet me at the train station, take me to my hotel, show me around town a bit, and take me to dinner on the waterfront.

I traveled light on the train. My only luggage was a leather hat box, two changes of outfits, and my diary. I checked a big suitcase all the way through. Later, I had the folks send my trunk with more clothes.

The Johnsons took good care of me. I looked up other old friends from Hollywood, and before long, news got around that I was in town. There were phone calls for interviews and social events. Life was beginning to perk. I stayed busy writing notes home, because this was my first time alone in the big world away from my parents.

The summer humidity really got it me, and I spent most of the mornings resting in my room. Around lunch, I'd go looking around the big town and tall buildings. It was easy to get around using the streetcars and buses. I'd often have lunch with friends. If nothing was going on, I'd go to Central Park and take my diary to record the exciting events of the day.

I met some theater people, all of whom were nice and receptive. There were groups of them who got together for dinner and dancing at the various nightclubs, and I was often included.

One evening, I was asked out by a popular stage actor and a group of theater folks. As we were dancing, we saw Howard Hughes twirling some gal on the floor. After going back to the table with my friends, my escort soon disappeared. He didn't return and we wondered what had happened to him. Soon, Howard Hughes walked over to our table and joined us. He was a very handsome young man at that stage in his life. It seems he had some friends in our group. The mystery of the evening unfolded.

My escort had been dating the girl Howard was with that night. They'd had a breakup, but when they saw each other there, they took off together, dumping Howard and me. Howard asked if he could join us and escort me for the rest of the evening. What an unusual turn of events. We all went to several other nightspots and had a great time. Howard was completely charming and fun to be with.

As the party wound up, Howard asked me to have dinner with him the next week. I accepted, but with some doubt that he would remember or even keep the engagement. I figured I'd be ready when the evening came, just in case.

On the night of our plans, Howard called a bit late and explained he had just flown in from someplace and had a forced landing on the beach and wouldn't be too presentable, so we would just have dinner.

He picked me up a bit disheveled and unshaven, but we went out and had a nice dinner and conversation. He brought me back to my hotel and was a perfect gentleman.

So much for my unusual introduction and date with Howard Hughes.

CHAPTER 17 | *Dear Abby*

Nothing was happening professionally in New York, but socially, I seemed to be busy. Some lady I'd met asked me for lunch to meet a friend of hers. His name was Abby Dreyfuss, a very handsome Jewish fellow in his late thirties, maybe forty. I was in my early twenties. He had just gone through a divorce after finding his wife cheating on him. He put her clothes in the elevator and sent her on her way.

So, Abby was looking and seemed to like what he saw in me. We had dinner every night at the Waldorf Astoria roof garden, where we danced to Xavier Cugat's band. On our first date, Abby sent a corsage of seven orchids on one stem. I was embarrassed and wouldn't pin it on. It was too much. I felt like a gangster's moll.

Abby was a fabulous dancer and one evening, he said, "Don't look now, but my ex-wife is out on the dance floor. Wait until she sees you!"

He had been hurt and was getting even in his own way.

Through the course of conversation, I learned Abby was fabulously wealthy. He was an only child, and there was just he and his mother; his father was deceased.

Abby also had a read on the stock market. His family owned buildings and all sorts of oil holdings in Texas.

We had only a few dates when he invited me to travel to Europe with him. He was already booked on the big *Normandy* ship for a trip to France. He said, "Baby, come with me."

I laughed and said something like, "Oh no. I couldn't jump off the boat and run." He took me with him to see him off, and I had a tour of the fabulous *Normandy*, which was like a floating hotel.

Abby left his chauffeur and car at my disposal. He really hated to leave me and he demonstrated just how much he'd miss me. After the boat tour and a tearful goodbye, his chauffeur drove me back to my hotel.

A big surprise was in store. The next day, a cable came from Abby. "I am returning right away," it read. "Wait for me!" He barely got off the boat in France when he decided he missed something me and had better hurry back on the *Normandy*. He cabled me all the way back. The excitement was mounting: "Don't eat." "Wait for me." "I have gifts."

It was all very flattering, but I wasn't swept off my feet by it all. I was cautious and not about to fall into a trap of what I suspected was a wealthy playboy's rebound.

The gifts he presented when he arrived were spectacular, of course. Among them was a gorgeous wristwatch of 72 diamonds. It was a stunner.

Abby was very attentive and extremely generous. At dinner, he would pull out a huge roll of bills and say, "I had a big day on the market. Help yourself, baby. Get something you'd like or pay your hotel bills." I'd shove the roll back to him and say, "No, thanks." He was accustomed to New York showgirls who were always on the take and ready to be staked. I was something different, not of that caliber. Abby didn't quite understand, but I guess he liked the difference.

I had been in New York about three months. I was having a great time, but nothing was happening professionally. I knew Abby thought a lot of me, but I was thinking of another direction—home! I was also pondering what I wanted from life. It surely wasn't to consider something serious or settling for a wealthy playboy. We had absolutely nothing in common.

Frankly, I was simmering down on New York and all the dinner, dancing, and dating with Abby. I also realized that he had his play time every afternoon during rendezvous with various showgirls. It all seemed empty and a waste of my time.

I'd had quite an education about men in the film industry, not only from actors, but from studio executives and others in the business. There was so much infidelity that I came to the conclusion that none of them could be trusted to be loyal to their mates. There was just too much beautiful and willing material running around, and men, by nature, are just too susceptible and easily attracted.

I even learned that these guys had girls imported from the Far East for their use, and some of the foreign stars were the private property of some film executives.

I am proud to say that the film work I got over my 25 or so years in the business I received on my own merit as a competent actress, not because I was involved with some director or producer. I'm sure many didn't believe that, but it's true. There were no scandals or gossip about me to be raked up. Even Walter Winchell, the chief Hollywood reporter of all gossip made the comment that, "Joyce Compton is the only decent girl left in Hollywood." Many would not have taken that comment as a compliment — I did!

That is not to say that many would have cornered me if they could. But, I had a cute way of cleverly sidestepping them in their approaches. I did it in a way that neither hurt their feelings nor damaged their egos. If some were pressing me for dates while I was working on a film, I'd say, "Oh, I never go out while I'm working. I have to concentrate and put all my energies into my role." I'd try to be warm and flattering in how I handled them.

After my role was finished and the picture wrapped, I'd be long gone and couldn't be found. They would be after someone else. I still had no trouble getting the work, because I did it well, even though I didn't play the game.

So many Jewish fellows seemed to be attracted to me. I'd say, "Mom, I seem to be a Jewish boy's dish, a tall blonde, full of sparkle and fun."

The one thing that I wanted more than anything in the world was a home of my own, one that I would design and build myself. Who had I met that would be substantial, secure, loyal, and dependable, truly caring about me as a person and not simply intrigued by the glamour of a movie career? And when that intrigue wore off, then what? Would any of this get me a home? Building a home of my own was truly my greatest desire, the only material thing I longed for. It meant more peace, happiness, and security than any man could give me, at least the men I'd met. I decided that if I was to ever have a house, I would have to get it myself.

This idea ran through my mind the last days of my New York adventure. I told myself I had to get myself back home and back to business. I would try and get all the film work I could do for as long my career held out. I was aware that the average film career was something like six years or so.

Abby was going on a short trip to Chicago to see his mother. Now was the time, I thought, to get out of town. No notice. No goodbyes. I packed up, bought a train ticket, and was soon on my way to California. There were Mom and Dad, and new goals and plans that didn't include Abby. I knew he would be surprised and perhaps feel as though he'd been dumped, but, with all he had on a string, he wouldn't be lonely.

My heart and mind felt lifted as the train trundled me homeward.

CHAPTER 18 | *Back to Work*

When I made that long trip back to Hollywood, I had one thing on my mind — getting back to work. I thought Abby was behind me, in the past. That hope turned out not to be so. In the meantime, I went right to work without missing a beat. It was as though I'd never been away.

At various times, I had used Ruth Collier and Al Kingston as agents. When I returned from New York, I signed with the Hallam Cooley Agency, the best of

Walter Catlett and me in Daddy Knows Best.

them all. He was so sold on me and my talent, and there wasn't much we went after that we didn't come away with.

In 1933, I signed with Mack Sennett, the King of Comedy, to play the ingénue in short subjects. His short subjects — I think I did about nine of them — were the perfect way to display my evolving flair for comedy. The films called for me to little more than stand around while the comedians got the laughs. Yet, they were good training.

Working at Sennett's was hard work. The exhausting work schedule, which included shorts with Sennett and roles in other features, took their toll on my strength, which was weak in the best of situations. Plus, the work was made more difficult by the casualness and the lack of organization at Sennett's studio.

A couple of years later, I worked in two-reelers with Charley Chase, another comedy legend. I think I did three shorts with him, *Manhattan Monkey Business* being my favorite of the batch, in particular the scene where we go to a swanky restaurant. In this one, he manages to get his hands sticky while eating Welsh rarebit, I think. When we get to the dance floor, he twirls me around, not realizing until it's too late that his hands have stuck to my dress. He rips the dress

Charley Chase rips the dress off in Manhattan Monkey Business.

from my body. I'm left mortified.

Working with Charley was fun, and he was a gentleman. His shop was operated in a more orderly manner and positive atmosphere than Sennett's. There was some talk of Charley's love of drink, but, when I knew and worked with him, he was a professional who knew his business. He died not long after of a heart attack.

Over at Paramount, I had a nice role in *If I Had a Million*, which turned out to be one of my favorites feature films. The story is told in segments. A wealthy man selects people at random for gifts of a million dollars each. The story follows these people and tells what happens with each person who received the money.

Lucien Littlefield played my dad. Our characters ran a hamburger stand. Along comes Jack Oakie and Gary Cooper as customers. The three of us flirt a bit and make a date for later. They had received a million dollar check. Believing the check to be phony, they give it to me. Coming for the date later, they find me all dolled up to the hilt in feathers and furs. I'd cashed the check, which I'd found to be the real thing.

Sing, Sinner, Sing and *Affairs of a Gentleman* were two fun films I did with Leila Hyams and Paul Lukas in 1933 and 1934. Now, *there* was a romantic

I ran a hamburger stand in If I Had a Million. *Here I am with Gary Cooper, Jack Oakie, and Roscoe Karns.*

Romeo (Lukas) who surely liked the ladies. He burned up my phone lines talking of a divorce from his wife. Such talk didn't mean a thing to me.

Unholy Love was another of the 13 films I did in 1933. A modern version of *Madam Bovary*, it had a superb cast that consisted of H.B. Warner, Lila Lee, Beryl Mercer, Jason Robards, Lyle Talbot, and that handsome roué Ivan Lebedeff.

When I went to interview for my role in *Unholy Love*, I wore a rather unusual design of mine. I call it a coat dress because it fastened and looked like a coat. I was in an office with the producer and director, who were doing the casting. They asked me to take off my coat. I couldn't, of course, with it being my whole outfit. "I can't take it off," I said. "I haven't anything underneath." The way I said it seemed to suit the character they were casting and I got a leading part. I consider it one of my best roles. In the film, I had a husband and a number of lovers. I believe I also committed suicide. It was a quite a departure from my comedy and the dumb blonde stuff.

Another casting change from my usual comedic work was my role as a student nurse in *The White Parade*, a picture that took me back to Fox. Loretta Young, the star of the picture, was one of the student nurses, along with Astrid Allwyn, June Gittleson, and Muriel Kirkland. Loretta was a nice person to work with. Oh, what a beautiful face that woman had! At the end of the picture, she gave a lovely Melbourne Spurr portrait, which she autographed, "Thank you, sugar."

With the handsome Ivan Lebedeff.

I had a small part in *The Trumpet Blows* over a Paramount. Although my role is forgettable, my memory of George Raft is firm. This was the first time I worked with that Romeo. We worked again together in *Manpower, You and Me,* and *They Drive by Night.*

George always had a group of men around him, sort of like gangster bodyguards. They even worked in his films so they could be close to him. I couldn't figure it out. George would send one of them to ask me for a date.

I'd smile and reply, "What's the matter, can't George ask for his own date?" Maybe he was afraid of being turned down, I don't know. I followed up with, "Tell George that I don't think I'm his type," meaning I wasn't a play girl. "I am a quiet home girl." George's hanger-on came back with, "Oh! George likes to stay home, too."

I found I was getting better roles than I'd ever had under contract, with all the star competition and politics one had to play. Things began to pick up. I found a niche in comedy and characterizations. The studios would say, "That's a Joyce Compton role; let's get her for the part." Or, if it was a part of no particu-

I play a student nurse in The White Parade *with Loretta Young (right) and Dorothy Wilson (center).*

lar interest in the film, they would say, "Let's get Joyce for the role; she will put the right amount of personality and sparkle into the film."

On many occasions in the early 1930s, in some of those B-pictures made at independent studios, I was in the company of long-time veterans, many of whom were stars in silent films: Lilyan Tashman, Lew Cody, Betty Blythe, Lila Lee, H.B. Warner, and Lois Wilson, for example. In other words, they were seasoned professionals who knew the motion picture business. We would get some inadequate director who didn't know what he was doing, much less be able to properly direct the cast. If we hadn't been trained and experienced enough to more or less take over and plan our scenes and work out our rehearsals, there wouldn't have been a finished picture. Some of these film experiences were circuses.

I would often wonder how a picture got finished when I'd hear writers,

George Raft and I in You and Me.

directors, and producers hassling and arguing over a script for hours, even days! Production would stop, the cast would wait. Maybe I'd memorize pages and pages of dialogue, only to have it all thrown out and replaced with pages of entirely new dialogue and action to be memorized in minutes. Throw out the old from my mind and pound in the new. Tough work! Talk about stress and tension, but all part of the acting profession in my day.

I learned to be a thorough and diligent study of my roles. "One-take Joycie," they used to call me. Extra takes cost money, so I was a money saver for them. Then, it was often a hassle and quite frustrating for everyone in a scene when a star or actor hadn't learned his lines and would repeatedly blow up over not knowing his part. There would be take after take until my own spontaneity was completely worn threadbare. In some cases, my best take was lost way back there in previous takes. The director would give up and yell, "Cut, print!"

CHAPTER 19 | # House Plans and a Final Abby Episode

In the middle of my film work, I got busy with house plans. My folks had been looking around in the area for some property. The Bank of Hollywood was working through their problems of how to divide up a few dollars and cents to all those who lost their fortunes.

We selected a piece of land, about three-fourths of an acre in a sparse area of Sherman Oaks, just south of Ventura Boulevard. We turned in our stock we'd had with the bank and made the purchase.

In the meantime, Abby held on. I immediately received telegrams from him when I returned from New York. "Why did you run? I was coming right back," he wrote.

We corresponded a bit, but I was working and had little thoughts of him. Out of nowhere, Abby informed me that his mother was coming our way and asked my parents and me to meet and entertain her. She was a very nice lady and seemed so interested in us. One could sense that she was anxious for Abby to settle down and get married.

Not long after his mother's visit, Abby announced he was coming to California and wanted to see me. Perhaps his mother had approved of the Comptons. On his arrival, he checked into the Ambassador Hotel, called and sent a cab for me to join him there. I let him know I was busy on a picture and didn't have dating time for him. Over the course of his visit, I told him of our plans to build a house in the Valley. He was jealous, knowing for sure he was out of the picture.

In New York, he had met a friend of mine who lived in Los Angeles. He looked her up while here and made numerous offers of expensive gifts if she would get us together. That was also a no-go!

His Plan B was the final straw. "Baby, let's take your little home and your lot in Sherman Oaks and put it all on a home for us in Beverly Hills," he proposed. The nerve this man had with his cheap selfishness, without any consideration for my parents and where they would live. And, with all his money, he wanted to take from me the little I had acquired.

He brought up a comment that I once made about quitting my work if I ever married, that marriage would be all the career I could or would want to handle. He said, "By all means, don't quit your film work." He wanted me to stay in it for the glamour and whatever I might earn.

I had heard it all and had had enough of Abby. I couldn't get rid of him fast enough. He wouldn't quit calling or pressing me. To get rid of him, I finally decided to package up his 72-diamond wristwatch and send it back to him. In my independence, I had never wanted gifts from anyone I didn't care for and I wanted him to know there wouldn't even be a friendship left for us.

My friends thought I was foolish, of course, and that he would just give the watch to some little tramp, which is exactly what he did.

I heard later that Abby had gotten into serious trouble with a young girl. He apparently knew someone in a prominent publishing family and was able to get out of it. He probably had to pay someone off, I don't know.

The last time I heard from him, he called with a downcast repentance. He also had the nerve to fling at me, "All the trouble I had was your fault, because you wouldn't come back to me."

And so, it was goodbye to ole Abby.

With all the experiences that had passed my way by now, marriage and men folk were about as far from my mind or plans as you could get. In fact, I hardly dated, for fear that if I became interested, I might not get my home built. This was my chief goal, aim, and purpose.

CHAPTER 20 | *How to Build a House from Scratch*

With Abby out of the picture, I focused on our three-fourths of an acre lot in Sherman Oaks. I began drawing plans for the house I wanted to build. Using an inch for a foot scale, I designed the Tudor-style house I envisioned. It had two stories and about 3,000 square feet. I calculated the details: the number of beams, fireplaces, windows, and doors. I even included the electrical outlets in my layout.

There was a huge stone fireplace and two large castle-style entrances. Three steps led to the dining room level, where, at either end, there were long panels of French windows and a double-door panel leading to a lounging and dining porch that ran the length of the house. Both the kitchen and dining room were in beautiful wood paneling. The kitchen had peasant-style art work on the cabinets. Behind the kitchen was a long porch for two refrigerators and laundry. Also, a maid's room and bath opened off one side of the porch.

Stairs came up from the side corner of the dining room, leading upstairs to the hallway. Dad's bedroom, linen closet, full bath and stall shower, and my bedroom opened off the front strip of the hall. Then, a couple of steps up to another level was Mom's bedroom. My room had gabled ceilings with great truss beams similar to a mountain lodge. The garage was underneath Dad's room.

I loved to sunbathe in the nude, so that my tan would have no clothing marks. I'd climb up a ladder to the flat roof of our bungalow. Well, in this house, I'd planned a large sundeck leading out of Mom's bedroom through French doors. I'd oil up and lie nude on a sun pad in complete privacy.

For a girl in her twenties with no formal architecture training, I think I did a pretty good job.

The Great Depression was still on, so it was the perfect time to start our project. Labor and materials were at an all-time low or we couldn't possibly have started.

Dad hired one fellow needing a job to help him measure, layout, and dig the foundation. He had taken my hand-drawn plans and had a blueprint made. Getting started with the foundation seemed to take an awfully long time. Now and then, Dad would bring Mom and me out to see the progress.

Sherman Oaks, even the entire Valley, was quite rural in those days, with a lot of rolling fields. We often wondered how we could have ever built if we hadn't had the whole area around to drive up with the loads of lumber, sand, cement, stone, brick, and all that was needed.

People who watched the progress said that Dad had built a foundation that could hold up a 10-story building.

After the foundation was in, the walls started going up. Loads of lumber were delivered. Now and then, when film work wasn't coming in, we had to say, "Sorry, fellas. We'll have to let you go until Joyce gets a job and a few more dollars to pay you." We were paying cash as we went along. There were no debts hanging over us. We couldn't have paid them if we had. We didn't have the security of a steady income, just a few incoming dollars as I got a job to eat on, put gas in the car, and pay the $50 a month mortgage on our little house. Carpenters were sad and desperate, as they waited for our calls to come back.

Dad would do what his hard-working hands could do until the carpenters could come back. So, dollar by dollar, board by board, brick by brick, we all worked on that home.

Dad was always discovering interesting things at thrift shops to pick up and use for the house when the time came. Items like a wrought-iron lantern, a metal latch, and old tools. He could make and turn out anything with his hands. He couldn't seem to make a living in more secure ways, but there was nothing else he couldn't do, or at least try.

So, days, weeks, and months went by with slow building. Our plan was to finish a certain part of the house so we could move in, close a door, and have roofing. We'd need to put in a phone for my calls, then work things out from there. Instead of driving back and forth from our little home in Glendale to the building site in Sherman Oaks and to and from the studios for work, it made better sense if we were all together in one spot.

We moved in our new home on May 1, 1935. The downstairs, with nothing but wall frames, was open, but two bedrooms of the three bedrooms upstairs were finished. We had our little bit of furniture delivered for about $25. We sat the baby grand piano downstairs underneath blankets to keep it free of sawdust.

Mom and I started keeping house, sweeping sawdust this way and that while the carpenters stayed busy sawing and hammering. We dreamed we would one day have rugs and drapes in their proper place.

When we first moved in, we were real pioneers. For months, there was no plumbing, electricity, or gas. We cooked on some stacked bricks in the yard and went to bed after our day's labor with our three coal oil lamps. We heated kettles of water for our big tin tubs to bathe in.

It was some accomplishment and a great relief when we could close in the bath area and get our plumbing equipment, sink, and pedestal tub in place. Then, when the kitchen stove could be hooked up and the gas was on, what convenience! When we got electricity, it was luxury, although the house was a long way from being finished.

So much for the life of a glamorous movie star, huh?

CHAPTER 21 | Rustling with the Cowboys

About the time we started on the construction of our home, I was cast with Johnny Mack Brown in *Rustlers of Red Dog*, a 12-part serial that is still quite popular with Western-film fans.

Most of the shooting was done on location at various scenic spots around the Los Angeles area. Locations were fun with long rides on horses into the woods. There were cowboys and Indians around wagons to stir the dust, which always

Charles K. French played my father in Rustlers of Red Dog.

ended up in our powder, powder puffs, and makeup.

I loved the Western costumes: full, long dresses for me and cowboy shirts and hats for Johnny. We made quite an attractive couple.

I'd known Johnny since we first worked together way back in the silent days in *Soft Living*, a Madge Bellamy vehicle at Fox. I knew him to be a man of high quality, a Southern gentleman from Alabama. Meanwhile, back on the ranch at Universal and on location for *Rustlers of Red Dog*, Johnny and I developed a cute and sweet relationship. It helped to warm and sparkle the long, hard days and hours of work. He would hurry in every morning, full of enthusiasm, and talk with me while wardrobe got me fixed in costumes and the hairdresser arranged my curls and bonnet.

"I just had to come and see how my girl is this morning," Johnny would say. So this went on for some weeks. Our romance was warm, but innocent. I thought it would be nice at the end of production, if we brought our civilian clothes, and for the first time, see each other out of our Western characters and as we were in natural life.

We changed in the studio dressing rooms at Universal and went to a popular nightclub on the Sunset Strip, where we had cocktails and dinner. We had fun just being ourselves, Joyce and Johnny, not Mary and Jack, our characters.

I assured Johnny that night on the town that our romance could go no fur-

With the popular cowboy, Tim McCoy, in Fighting for Justice.

ther. No phone calling or making contact. I told him to go home to his family, be a good boy, and forget about me.

He wangled later to have me in another film, *Valley of the Lawless*, and he wanted to make us a team in some of his Westerns. I wasn't interested. Westerns were too hard and unrewarding work for a girl. All the glory goes to the male or his horse — or something! Not the girl. So, I bowed out of anything further.

A few years ago, I was out at the Motion Picture Hospital visiting someone and heard that Johnny was there and not too well. I went in to see him briefly. Poor dear, he was old, ill, and quite heavy, going the way of all flesh. He passed on shortly after.

Westerns were not my cup of tea, so to speak, but work was work, and I was pleased to have a job. Some of them were better than others.

Some years later, I was back at Republic filming *Silver Spurs* with Roy Rogers and Phyllis Brooks. I enjoyed the trip and time we were on location in Kernville, California. We filmed our scenes in a very scenic spot on the Kern River.

Our accommodations were in motel-type bungalows. There was some knocking on of doors every evening by a singing cowboy who wanted to come in and rehearse the script. Phyllis and I smiled, but didn't open the door. Roy had his wild days before settling down into his great marriage with Dale Evans. They later became two of my closest friends.

CHAPTER 22 | # The Lear Jet Set and Other Hollywood Adventures

With a house of our own, built to my specifications, I was free to concentrate on my career. By the mid-1930s, my reputation as a comedienne, perhaps of the dumb Southern blonde type, was intact. It was during this time, from 1935 to the early 1940s, that I did some of my best film work. But, make no mistake: I was anything but dumb off the screen.

I was pretty well educated by now on how things operated in Hollywood, especially with the male species and the additional expectations that came along with working in the picture business. From time to time, I did, as you know, get myself into some pickles.

For instance, there was an experience with a big agent — his name is not important. He had a deal where he signed actors and actresses to personal contracts and paid their salaries. He loaned — or sold — them to various studios for film roles. Sounds like the oldest profession, doesn't it?

I was called into his office for an interview regarding such an arrangement. I had never met the man before, but certainly knew of him. Getting to his office late in the day (my first mistake), he said he had to run out to his home for something and asked me to come with him. We could talk things over there.

Not wanting to appear like an unsophisticated kid, I agreed (my second mistake). In my defense, I have to say that, as we left the office, there was nothing said or done that caused me alarm. He appeared okay and on the up and up.

We drove way out in a rather sparsely-built area of sumptuous homes. His home and furnishings were gorgeous. He talked about his business arrangements. There was a housekeeper around, but she soon left. We were alone. He fixed his drink and I sipped on something. Then, he spilled his drink on his clothing and left to change into something more comfortable. That something more comfortable was a robe!

I began to smell a rat and got quite uneasy. It was getting to be evening and here I was in this isolated area and no place to go if I got out of the house. I recognized I was in a pickle and would have to figure a way out.

He wasn't advancing on me like a rapist, but I recognized his intent and didn't want to act like a scared kid. He talked of going to dinner and returning to his place. I decided I'd better be a clever actress.

I knew he had been drinking, but didn't know then that he was the type of alcoholic who went on binges for weeks. He didn't appear to be in any dangerous condition. I convinced him I had to make an appearance at home to my mother before going to dinner.

He was okay to drive. I was so relieved when we got into Sherman Oaks. I told my mother in private what was going on. Mom invited him to stay while she fixed some dinner and coffee to sober him up. With that done, he came to his senses, and went on his way. We got rid of him.

After my work in *Rustlers of Red Dog*, I was back at Republic in 1936 with a leading role in *Country Gentlemen*, starring the great comedy team, Ole Olsen and Chic Johnson. They had been together in vaudeville since the mid-1910s and had done only a few films. *Country Gentlemen* was their first at Republic. They knew little of film technique, only stage and vaudeville-type work.

They were great guys. Chic was the wild one, I guess. Ole was a quiet family man. We had quite a time working out our scenes. It took double and triple rehearsals and retakes to get the shots. The directors, Ralph Staub and Phil Ford, eventually frustrated with the team, would say, "Now, guys, watch this girl work and see how she does things."

We finally got a wrap on the picture. I don't remember whether I ever saw the film, but I surely remember the hard work and struggle I had with Ole and Johnson, not to mention a Great Dane I had to work with.

I became acquainted with Ole's daughter, Moya, during the filming. We became close friends and I was around the family for many years after that film experience.

Moya and I were into ice skating and I believe Ole had bought a nice open-air rink in Westwood. They had sort of a weekly open house that included swimming and barbecues. I was there many, many Sundays.

Moya was single, and somewhere along the way, fell in love with Bill Lear, of Lear Jet fame. He was older and married! Her family did all they could to break up the relationship. They even sent her to Europe for a change of atmosphere. It was a no-go. Lear finally divorced and he and Moya married. Bill had several older children. Then, he and Moya had a batch of their own. As she would say, "I was pregnant the first few years of our marriage." I stayed in touch with Moya, writing her during this time and visiting them at their home in Santa Monica when their new arrivals came.

Lear was a character and quite a genius. And, what a sense of humor that man had. They had a daughter named Shanda, so her full name became Shanda Lear!

They eventually bought a house in Toluca Lake across from other friends of mine, including violinist Duci De Kerekjarto, who had a home on the lakefront. I was with Duci and family a lot in those days and loved to fish in the lake in front of their house.

Anyway, Moya and Bill Lear's marriage was strong. She held things together and was a fabulous woman, wife, and mother. It seems that when Bill passed some years ago, she carried on his business and became successful in that. What a woman!

I had gone with a friend to a swanky party at the home of Eddie Hillman, a wealthy Beverly Hills playboy. Eddie had been married to some little starlet — maybe her name was Marion — but they had divorced and I guess he was playing the field.

All kinds of film personalities were at this party and a good time was being had by all. During the evening, Hillman and a group decided to go to Santa Barbara for a couple of days to attend a tennis tournament. I was one of those invited. Eddie, as I recall, was footing the bill for everyone.

I packed my bags and told the folks I was off to Santa Barbara. After we arrived, everyone was appointed to their accommodations. It was at one of those big hotels in Santa Barbara that had bungalows all over the grounds. Eddie reserved these for our party.

Everyone dressed in evening attire and went to the hotel for dinner. I found out I had been invited as Eddie's date and that he was sharing the other part of our bungalow. The common area, the living room, was between our suites.

After dinner, I found that Eddie had hired a big band. Everyone there was instructed to come to his living room to proceed with partying for the rest of the night. A bar was set up with bartenders and the works, and the band played on. The racket, talk, and laughter were deafening. They were all whooping it up!

I decided I'd had enough of this. I slipped away from it all, locked my door, and retired for the evening. Eddie had other girls and friends to keep him busy. I went to bed in my lounging pajamas and robe.

After awhile, there was a knock at my door. I ignored it, but soon, another knock. Eddie wanted me for something. I opened the door. He wanted me to take all his money, his wristwatch, and jewelry for safekeeping. He said I was the only one he trusted. I put it all under a blanket on a closet shelf.

Things would settle down for a short time. Then, he'd knock and call for me to let him in. During the trip up from Los Angeles, he'd picked up a little dog and he wanted me to keep it in my room. There was just no rest or peace for me.

Finally, the evening was closing down — it was towards morning — and Eddie came to my door wanting money to pay the band. Everyone had gone, and I figured Eddie would be all worn out, go to bed, and forget about me. After a while, he knocked and called for me again. I ignored him. I wasn't about to open my door with everyone gone. He left and I thought, "Oh, I can sleep now." I was so exhausted and in a haze and daze for sleep.

Suddenly, I heard the crash of breaking glass. There were French doors in my room that led to the hotel grounds. This idiot had gone outside and was breaking the glass into my room. In a panic, I raced from my bed, dashed into the bathroom, and locked the door. I had put the dog in there earlier to keep it from ruining the floor.

Eddie banged on the door and said for me not to be foolish and to come out. I stayed quiet and figured he'd leave. He did, and all got quiet. The next thing I heard was something tearing through the bushes by the bathroom window. It was Wildman Eddie back and crawling towards the window. He began to plead with me to come out. I was crying by this point. I told him I was afraid of him.

Eddie seemed to have some compassion and reassured me that he would go away and wouldn't bother me again if I would come out and go to bed. That seemed to settle the issue for that night, at least.

The next day, everyone was up and about, swimming, playing tennis, and enjoying a luncheon buffet. Eddie didn't bother me. He seemed to be enjoying himself with the others he brought on this jaunt.

We stayed in Santa Barbara for whatever festivities were being planned. The band came back for more entertaining at the bungalow. I didn't even attempt to retire. I stayed dressed in my white lace evening gown. It was one of my designs and fit like the paper on a wall, as they all did!

At the party, Eddie paid me no special attention, as the other girls seemed to fawn over him. As usual, the evening began turning into morning. I think it was Eddie who came up with a wild idea. A fellow in the party was more or less in a stupor after too much to drink. Eddie thought it would be a great prank to call an ambulance and haul the fellow off.

The ambulance came and the drunk began to come to and sober up. Eddie paid the ambulance extra and decided the whole group should climb aboard the ambulance and head somewhere for breakfast.

I had met a boy in the party who seemed to be a more reserved and quiet person, like myself. He had been attentive during all this craziness. When the gang left in the ambulance, I sidestepped it all and decided I'd never be missed. I stayed at the bungalow. The boy also stayed behind. As we stood there relieved that the rest of the guests had gone, we embraced and started kissing. Suddenly, the boy was knocked in the head and tumbled across the room in pain and shock. Eddie was back!

In all the excitement of leaving in the ambulance, Eddie realized that I wasn't with them and he called for a return to the bungalow. He walked in at the moment we started kissing and attacked the boy with a demonic force. It's a wonder the boy didn't receive a concussion from the blow. He then dashed at me, and with great force, shoved me backwards. I fell over the foot of the bed, cutting my legs. Blood spattered all over my white dress. The rest of the guests — Eddie's attorney was one of them — came in and witnessed the whole scene. The attorney reminded me that, before we left Los Angeles, he had informed me about Eddie's radical activities and instability.

This incident wound up the party, and we soon packed up and returned to Hollywood. The dog he asked me to keep did indeed mess up the carpet and Eddie had to pay for the repairs. He also brought the dog with us in the car on the way home. Eddie had a gun, and although others in the car were trying to calm him, he shot at random out the car window along the Pacific Coast Highway from Santa Barbara to Los Angeles.

CHAPTER 23 | *Cary Grant and "The Awful Truth"*

My role as Dixie Belle Lee in *The Awful Truth*, made in 1937 for Columbia, is one of my most memorable roles. It's the one my fans seem to remember most. Dixie Belle is a nightclub singer who tries to help Cary Grant get over his ex-wife, played by the lovely Irene Dunne.

Cary had a crush on me — or something! He took the ringside seat on the set every time I did my scene in a nightclub in which I sang the line, "My dreams

Cary Grant and I in a scene from The Awful Truth.

are gone with the wind." At that point, a blow machine would billow my full skirt into the air and reveal lots of leg. Maybe Cary was a leg man, I don't know.

Sometime after we made *The Awful Truth*, I was dating some fellow from the studio. He invited me to go to a party at the beach home of Cary and Randolph Scott. When we got there, all kinds of film people were milling about. Everyone was having fun in the large pool, on the beach, and in the ocean. There was a big spread of food and drinks for everyone.

Shortly after we arrived, my escort said he had to leave, but that I should stay at the party. He said I'd be okay and would have fun with the guests. I learned later that Cary had set this ploy into motion. They had decided my escort would bring me to the party, then leave. This rather set me back. I didn't like it. I felt like I'd been procured.

Cary was around and about with everyone, not just centering on me. And, as I continued to catch on to his plot, I didn't particularly give him a tumble of flattering attention. He didn't know what to say to me and stumbled even trying to get his words out. He probably thought I'd be overwhelmed and just fall into arms and stay the night.

Well, he had the wrong idea! I'd only met him on the film and worked with him in a few scenes. We didn't know each other at all. There wasn't enough between us to even spark a flirtation.

As the afternoon wore on, I wondered how I would get home. Cary came around and said he was going upstairs to shave. "Maybe you'll like me better then," he said.

When he left, I decided to talk to another girl there whom I knew and had worked with. She seemed to be getting a bit tipsy. Hal Roach was there and was amusing himself by standing my friend on her head, so I figured she needed to get out, too. I asked her to take me with her to her home and then I'd call my dad to pick me up there. The deal was made. I'd probably made a rescue for her, as well as myself.

Cary came down all shaven and ready for whatever, but not ready to see me leaving. He was crestfallen and taken aback as I thanked him for my lovely day.

Sometime later, I ran into Cary again, and he commented that he was in love with me at that time and didn't know how to become acquainted. He had called Hal Roach to find me and arranged for the fellow to invite me down to the beach. Anyway, it worked out for the best. In love with me? I'd simply say, "Just a passing attraction watching my dress fly up over my head!"

CHAPTER 24 | The Glamorous and Bejeweled Chickie

My work in *The Awful Truth* got me more work than I could hardly handle. I think I made 12 pictures that year. *Spring Madness*, in which I play one of Maureen O'Sullivan's matchmaking sorority sisters, was a good role.

I brought out the glamour as Chickie in *Artists and Models Abroad*. Working with Jack Benny and Mitchell "Mitch" Leisen, the director, was a delight. Some of my best glamour photos and stills came from that picture.

Wearing the stunning outfit Mitch Leisen designed for me in Artists and Models Abroad.

Mitch Leisen designed my black jersey evening gown and big "picture" hat with real Bird of Paradise feathers and gold gauntlet gloves. The dress fastened down the center front with real jewel fastenings. I also wore a genuine jeweled bracelet. The jewelers stayed on the set to protect and insure their property. I'd take the jewels off when we went to lunch and was dressed on camera for my scenes, as all the models were.

With that cute Walter Pidgeon in Sky Murder.

Mitch had a cute comment as he watched the girls being dressed. Those who were not well-endowed were stuffed with padding. Mitch said, "I never saw such a bunch of tit-less wonders!"

Jack Benny was a dear man, and we had so many laughs together on that film. He seemed to like me and said I had a cute nose. He followed me around looking at it and calling me Chickie. I heard later his wife, Mary Livingstone, had her nose bobbed, maybe in the Joyce Compton style!

My role as female detective Christine (Chris) Cross in *Sky Murder* was one of my best, if not my best, role. I appeared opposite Walter Pidgeon, who was making his third and last film as detective Nick Carter. Walter was a handsome old roué and awfully cute, too.

He used to follow me around and try to catch me for a kiss in the hallway outside our dressing rooms. He would say, "Oh, if I were only a pretty young girl who knew what men want, I'd never have to work again and I'd have everything I could want."

CHAPTER 25 | *The Fur Flies*

Turnabout, made in February 1940, was another fun and enjoyable role. I was part of the stellar cast that included Adolphe Menjou, Mary Astor, Carole Landis, William Gargan, John Hubbard, Verree Teasdale, Donald Meek, Inez Courtney, and Marjorie Main. Did they come any better than that?

One of the reasons I liked the role of Irene Clare is because, like Chickie in *Artists and Models Abroad*, she was dressed to the hilt in designer clothes, hats,

Wearing the fur coat from Turnabout *that caused such a ruckus.*

and furs. They even designed a fur muff for me to carry around one of my Griffons, which they rented for various scenes in the picture.

My favorite wrap was a fur evening cape with a deep yoke in the front and hand embroidered and jeweled in the back. It was designed especially for me. Needless to say, it was stunning!

After the picture wrapped, we were allowed to purchase some items that had

Clowning around with Carole Landis (center) and Mary Astor on the set of Turnabout.

been designed for us. So, I had my eye on that fur coat. Over the years, I had acquired a rather nice wardrobe, which made me a stunner for nights on the town. I also used pieces of my own personal wardrobe in some of the films I made at independent studios. Then again, if it was a major studio that didn't want the expense of designing my whole wardrobe for the picture, they would rent some of my own personal clothing for me to wear. It supplemented my income.

Anyway, I had spoken for this particular coat, but it remained at the studio until the possibility of retakes was over. At that point, I picked up the coat and paid the studio. It found its new home in my wardrobe. I considered it settled.

Imagine my surprise when various individuals from Hal Roach's studio began bombarding me with calls. They wanted the coat back. If it had been for retakes or such, of course I would have brought the coat back for that use. It seemed, however, that Hal Roach's daughter, Margaret, had borrowed the coat from the wardrobe department before my purchase. She had worn it to parties and told everyone her mother had gotten it for her birthday.

Margaret also called wanting the coat. They even called my agent to put the thumbscrews on me. My agent advised me to give it up for fear it would knock me out of work at Roach's studio. I felt this was just too much pressure and harassment from people who could have had and afforded six coats just like it, or any fur coat, for that matter. So, I held my ground and refused to give it up.

Right or wrong, I still have that fur coat hanging in my closet. When I go to a friend's house for holiday dinners and such festivities, I jazz up their party by wearing my prize fight coat, as I call it.

Now that I think about it, I guess they made good on their promise. I don't think I ever worked for Hal Roach again.

The studio designed a fur muff for my Griffon.

CHAPTER 26 | *I Keep my Bangs*

By the early 1940s, I had been in the business for 15 years. Like the episode with the fur coat from *Turnabout*, I said what was on my mind and stood up for myself. This was Hollywood; I had no choice. Few others would speak up for you.

There were always petty things, such as hairstyles or costumes, being brought up to hassle you. For instance, if a star didn't want you dressed a certain way, the

Marlene and I with our bangs in Manpower. *Pictured (left to right): Lucia Carroll, Eve Arden, Marlene Dietrich, Lynn Baggot, and me.*

director or producer might ask you to change. This sort of thing happened when I was filming *Manpower.*

The star of the picture, the glamorous Marlene Dietrich, took one look at me and told the studio brass that she didn't want me to wear bangs because she intended to wear them in the picture. I had always worn bangs. They were part of the Joyce Compton look. Raoul Walsh, the director, was sent to ask me to change. The producer, Hal Wallis, I think, was called in to persuade me.

Finally, Dietrich herself faced me, and there was quite a scene between us. I talked my way through it. I said, "Marlene, dear, your bangs are of the more glamorous type, while mine are short, kid bangs." She finally gave up and I kept my bangs. She didn't seem to harbor any resentment toward me. She was quite the glamour girl who liked to have things her way.

With George Raft as her leading man in the picture, I've often wondered why Marlene didn't send Raft's shady entourage out to convince me to give up the bangs!

CHAPTER 27 | *"A Southern Yankee" and Some of the Men in my Life*

After we got into our house, there was still much work to be done. When not working around the house or at the studio on a film, I painted canvases. I did landscapes, self-portraits, and portraits of such stars as Clark Gable, Elizabeth Taylor, Marlene Dietrich, and Cary Grant. Our walls and easels were filled with my work.

For quite a while, I gave up dating for fear of having to eventually give up my home for the risky business of marriage. I made exceptions along the way. William Wyler and I dated some in the 1940s, but it was nothing serious. I had known him way back in the early part of our careers when he directed me in *The Border Cavelier*. I worked with him again in *The Best Years of our Lives* in the mid-1940s.

When we went to dinner, Willie seemed to always raise a ruckus over the food, the service, or something. So, I stopped going out with him. He kept calling and I wouldn't talk with him. Finally, Mom told him, "Joyce doesn't care to go out anymore." He couldn't understand why. Mom answered frankly, "That's just the way she is, if she's made up her mind about someone."

Mom had been having some serious health problems along the way. She had high blood pressure, which caused her heart to become enlarged. She ate too much, was too heavy, worked too hard, and was a worrier.

Often these spells would come in the night. I was so on the alert, that if I heard a sound from her in her bedroom, I'd be up in a flash and hurry to her side with my bottle of ammonia and smelling salts. I'd often fix ice bags to put on her chest to ease her pains or to her head for her blood pressure. I'd surely become a nurse on duty a good deal of the time.

I would often jump up so fast that I would become faint. When I got to her and was waving the bottle under her nose, I began to get woozy and grabbed the bottle for myself.

Mom noticed I was having trouble and began to worry. I thought it wouldn't do for me to be laid out over her, so I ran up to call for Dad. When I reached the hall, I blacked out completely, and fell into the corner of a table, tearing a gash in my head. When I came to, Mom and Dad were standing over me. Dad tried to lift me up. Mom told him to leave my head down so the blood would circulate. Getting Mom back in bed and me in mine, poor Dad ran back and forth with the bottle of smelling salts.

When we got up the next morning, we faced another impasse. Dad was hemorrhaging from the nose. He'd been struggling for some hours trying to use icepacks to stop the bleeding. We called our doctor, but he was busy with an emergency. Mom and I couldn't drive and get him to the hospital. We knew no one to help. Dad got weaker and weaker and lost a lot of blood.

Always on our own, we had never had anyone to rely on but one another.

I had just met someone a short time before, a fellow named Avis. My friend of some years, Rosalie, had taken me out to John Carroll's home. Avis was staying as a houseguest after getting out of the service as Captain Avis Blackman.

We called Avis and he came. Our doctor finally called an ambulance for Dad to be admitted to the hospital. Avis drove Mom and me. They cauterized a vessel in his nose and barely saved his life. Avis made himself available to take us to the hospital to see Dad. What a help and blessing he was.

Mom fixed a great dinner for Avis every evening after coming home from the hospital. He, too, loved food and was a big eater. Dad finally came home, but was in a weakened condition. He was ordered to stay in bed.

With Red Skelton in A Southern Yankee.

In the meantime, I was cast in *A Southern Yankee*, as a brunette belle who tries to entice Red Skelton. It was a great role for me and another of my favorite parts. With Dad unable to drive me to MGM every day, whom did we turn to, but Avis. He was more than pleased to be available to me.

He picked me up every morning and drove me over the mountains and down into Culver City and MGM. He came to see me at lunch, brought his camera, and took color photographs of me. I wore a Southern Belle dress and a black wig for the part. I was quite fetching.

I'd call Mom to let her know what time I'd be home and she would have a hot meal waiting on us when we arrived. Avis was totally intrigued by now and sort of becoming part of the family.

He was born in Tel Aviv, Israel, and we knew he was Jewish. For some reason, he told us he was German and Egyptian and that his family had a plantation and grew crops in Egypt. We didn't care about any of that or what he told us. We were just fond of him and his great kindness to us. Mom's cooking and being with me had won his heart. I realized that I had sometimes been picky about some of my dates, so Mom and I decided to bend over backwards to like and appreciate him.

When *A Southern Yankee* was finished and Dad had somewhat recuperated, Avis continued to come over many evenings with ice cream or watermelon. He would sit on the side porch and tell his war stories of being with General Dillon in the Criminal Investigation Division (CID). He tried writing some of his experiences in an effort to interest some of the studios. I introduced him to some in the writing departments at various studios, but nothing came of his efforts.

We began to find out that Avis was quite a fabricator about many of the things he'd been telling us. He didn't mind making up an untruth, it seemed, about most anything. So, we tried to overlook and ignore his stretches of the truth.

A 1945 publicity shot.

Once, he presented me an engraved Petik Felipe watch and two stunning jeweled rings. He had written a story about them and their background, which he read to us at dinner one evening. We later found out there had been a big jewel robbery during the war and the CID had solved the case. Apparently, he had helped himself to a few of the pieces.

At one point, Avis's conscience began bothering him about his alleged German-Egyptian background. Through other friends, I think he found out that we knew of his Jewish heritage. He asked to come and make a big, dramatic confession to us. We listened politely and Dad told him that none of it mattered to us and that he only cared about how he treated me.

Avis had it in his mind that we would eventually marry. I couldn't afford to have him reaching for this, so I began cutting back from seeing him. I was busy with work and Mom was having more health problems.

After not seeing him for some time, Avis called to see whether we could get back together. I told him it was better that we didn't see each other. He asked for the return of the rings. He told me to keep the engraved watch. I packaged them up, insured them, and dropped them in the mail.

I heard later that he had a fall, hurt his back, and eventually died from that injury.

My wonderful Mom, my rock of Gibraltar, began having more and more spells. One night, I rushed into her room I found her on the floor. As I helped her up, something passed over her body and face. I screamed for Dad to come. Mom was having a stroke. Our doctor came over and he and Dad lifted Mom to her bed.

I had a steady patient then. The doctor came occasionally to give a shot, and prescribe various medications. He left instructions for me to carry on.

I evidently did a good job. We were fortunate that Mom wasn't completely paralyzed. Her right side was paralyzed, however, and there were things she couldn't do for herself.

Mom's stroke was a sobering blow in my life. She had always been there for me in every need I had. I'd depended on her for so much. Now, she depended on me.

I wasn't the same Joycie after this. I'd always been more or less carefree, thanks to all the help my family had given me over the years. I was always full of laugher and fun at the studios and tried to make others happy. Now, I was serious and that happy side was sobered down. I was more conscious of my responsibility towards my wonderful parents.

Mom was in bed for several months. Dad was a big help to me. When we could get Mom up, we would wrap a rug around the legs of a straight chair, so she could stand, hold to the back, and push herself around the room.

She and Dad were close during this critical time. They had their bickering at times through the years, but now he was more patient and understanding of her. Mom had always looked to me, not Dad, for companionship, happiness, and security. Dad did his own thing and had his interests. Now, Mom depended on him more. They would sit together in the evening while he did therapy on her damaged hand and arm.

Picture jobs, my bread and butter over the years, were slowing down. There was only occasional work, as television was the new medium. So, I was more help with Mom. I helped her dress and fix her hair and face when needed. I never could kill a chicken or any of our yard fowls like Mom could, so Dad did her job and I'd do the rest. Mom would instruct me about how to cut up a newly-plucked chicken.

We always found something to laugh about. I remember when we figured the best way to get her on the bed pan. One time, we forgot that combination and were in hysterics rolling her body weight this way and that.

While she was at my mercy about her eating — I kind of put her on a diet, I really did her some good in the nutrition area. How mad she would get when I'd bring her a tray of healthy food, instead of what she wanted. She would fuss and say, "Just wait until I get up and get to that kitchen and fix what I want."

Our family structure seemed to be changing more and more. My parents were becoming my children and I the head of the house. I made decisions and was in charge of things.

About this time, someone new came into my life. Some friends introduced me to a very nice man who was some years older than me. He was fifty or so. I had never gone out with an older man, but I sort of liked it. His name was Walter and he was quite a successful building contractor. We dined at big hotels and the best restaurants and took trips to Palm Springs and Lake Arrowhead. I loved taking color photographs wherever we went and he got me a nice 35-millimeter camera that took color slides. I thoroughly enjoyed all his pampering. He was up for anything I wanted to do or any where I wanted to go.

Mom seemed so pleased that I had someone nice to go out with and also could do nice things for me. She liked Walter a lot.

What did I know about Walter when I met him? I knew he had been married, had two teenage sons, and that their mother had been killed in a car accident.

We dated steadily for a few months. I had all my nice wardrobe and glamour clothes, so I was all set for this attention. Walter was thrilled with the movie gal he had found.

Finally, he opened up and told me some things about his life. He was usually a very quiet person and rarely expressed anything about himself. "Walter, you don't talk to me or say how you feel about anything," I said. I began feeling I like I was sitting in a beautiful Cadillac or having a luxury dinner with a generous man that I knew nothing about. There wasn't much depth or interchange of understanding between us.

His answer to all this was, "If I talked, you wouldn't like me." Then, he lowered the boom. He told me he had had two marriages since his wife's death and the last one wasn't too long before he met me. I felt a big letdown as I heard all

Modeling for Walter at Lake Arrowhead.

of this. I had vaguely considered what it would be like to be married to a pampering, ever-loving, and father figure. I analyzed what might take place with my own family.

I could never walk away or desert my family. I'd dream up an idea. Walter and his sons lived a ways from me in a small town outside of Los Angeles. So, his situation wouldn't fit into mine or home life with my family. I wanted the home I'd longed for and built, and I couldn't move far away from aging and ill parents.

I got to thinking about Walter building a beautiful home that we would plan together, maybe near my home where I could keep tabs on the folks. I never really considered what it would be like to be stepmother to two teenage boys. Having to share someone's father sort of took the bloom out of anything romantic.

When he told me about the two other marriages, and especially the story of the last one, my thoughts changed color. I no longer considered marriage to this man.

Walter had had such a deep love, or perhaps it was more of a sick infatuation. He was consumed with his last wife, he said. He couldn't get over her. The girl was a glamorous little nightclub singer. In the short course of things, she drank, cheated on him, beat him up, and even cut up his clothes. It was really a nightmare this man had stepped into. He divorced her, but continued to be at her beck and call. She took advantage of him by running to him for her every need. It's no surprise that he developed ulcers over this woman.

When Walter finished his confessions and turned the conversation towards me and our possible marriage, I told him that because of my religious beliefs, I couldn't marry a man with two failed marriages. He was disappointed, but didn't need any more hurt or letdowns. We continued dating a few more months. I was totally satisfied with the company of a sweet and generous man.

Soon, Walter stopped calling. I waited, then called him to see what had happened. He said, "I don't feel we should go on seeing each other if there is no future for us." Bang! There it was! I had never been the one to be left. I'd always done the breaking up.

For a while, I admit that I was thinking selfishly and only of myself. He should have been glad I wasn't reaching for marriage, as most girls were, and was just satisfied with dating. He had a nice girl to take out and show off. He should have been satisfied. I knew better later on. This poor man surely didn't need more heartache and disappointment in his life.

I missed Walter terribly and was deeply grieved for a long time at this loss. Poor Mom cried and carried on over the separation much more than I. For me, it was time to move on.

CHAPTER 28 | # Forming the Hollywood Christian Group

For some years, my parents and I had attended the First Presbyterian Church on Gower Street in Hollywood. We attended on Sundays and usually on Wednesday evenings for supper and Bible study.

My parents would go to the older group, and I usually went to the college group where young folks were so inspired by our wonderful teacher, Henrietta Mears.

The Hollywood Christian Group was formed through Miss Mears, Dr. Erwin Orr, and a few film people. Its purpose was to reach people in all branches of the film industry. Anyone, actors or directors or electricians, anyone holding a Guild card, was eligible to be members.

Colleen Townsend, a sweet, young starlet at Fox, usually met with the college group at church and invited me to be part of the formation of the Hollywood Christian Group. "You must come and join with us," she said. "You are just what we need, a Christian actress who knows and has worked with so many big stars in the film industry. You can make such wonderful contacts and invite those you work with to the meetings we'll be planning." So, I got a job.

I was excited about the potential it promised for me to be able to use my Christian faith at the studios and the wonderful outlet and interest it would offer for fellowship among those we would bring into the group from our own film background.

We found that some church groups were so holy that they looked down on film players. Some considered us untouchable and often pulled their spiritual skirts aside from any real association with us. To them, we were unclean or not really Christian.

Mom and I would often invite young ministers to our home for dinner. They would enjoy the change from all their evangelizing and would sort of let their hair down. They enjoyed meeting a film personality and seeing my movie stills and such. While they may have been against me working in the film industry, they were always ready to come for that Southern feast Mom prepared and would call and invite some of their friends to join in.

One time, a certain evangelist friend I knew was to hold a meeting in a Long Beach church. The pastor of this church and his wife were also friends of mine. I thought it would be fun for Dad to drive me down to Long Beach, where I could get a hotel room and stay a few days, attend the meetings, and see the pastor and his wife.

I got settled in my room. Dad returned home, so I had no transportation. That first evening, I was heading to the meeting. I got on the elevator. There stood the evangelist I was going to hear.

I told him I was in town to hear him and asked him to give me a ride to the church. I guess he was trapped and had to agree. We chatted along the way. As we neared the church, he said, "Joyce, I'm going to ask you to get out of the car before we reach the front of the church. People would talk if they saw me drive up with you." I had to appear understanding, so I complied. However, I felt like dirt or a scarlet woman, anything but a nice person who happened to work in the film industry.

When the meeting was over, the pastor and his wife invited the evangelist and me to dinner. At the table, the issue was brought up about the evangelist and me staying at the same hotel. The preacher said it was best if he moved to another hotel. I protested, saying that I should be the one who moved, "since I seemed to be the problem." He moved to another hotel. I called Dad the next day to come and take me home.

So, the Hollywood Christian Group was to be a spiritual haven where I could practice my faith and be who I was. All of us took an active interest in certain areas. I wrote letters and invited others to come and join us. We hosted a big banquet and invited a few hundred new prospects. We rented a banquet room and had speakers like the Rev. Billy Graham and others for the evening.

We elected new presidents every year and formed a board of directors. Tim Spencer, one of the Sons of the Pioneers, was one of the first. His song, "Room Full of Roses," had been a big hit. Roy Rogers and Dale Evans also took their turn in presiding over the group.

The group often met in members' homes or on their lovely lawns during the hot summer evenings. Francis Eilers, wife of Leonard Eilers, the cowboy evangelist, was in charge of refreshments. Leonard would preach while twirling his cowboy ropes.

We sometimes met at the homes of Jane Russell, Rhonda Fleming, and Connie Haines. Many had enough room to house the group and they generously offered us their homes for our weekly meetings.

Once a year, we had a retreat at Forest Home, a lovely lodge with rustic cabins in the San Bernardino Mountains.

Colleen Townsend met and started dating the son of Dr. Louis Evans, a renowned preacher who was key in helping to support and expand the Hollywood Presbyterian Church. I saw them growing closer and soon they announced their marriage intentions after one of these retreats. When they married, she gave up her film career to be by her husband's side in his ministry.

Needless to say, with all I had going on at home with my parents, the Hollywood Christian group was my chief interest, outlet, and lifesaver from week to week. I had many home duties to attend to and provided care for my poor broken Mom. Her whole personality had changed. There was very little of left of her old self and all the joy and fun we'd had through my busy film years. I really missed the companionship we'd had.

CHAPTER 29 | *I Become a Prisoner*

Mom continued having a hard time in her life. Her battle was our battle, seeing her health declining while she was only in her sixties. She clung to life and to me, hating to give me up. I guess I was the only happiness she had really ever had. Getting her dressed in some pretty clothes and a big hat and going out to a nice lunch or dinner were her happiest moments.

One summer, I met and started dating a fellow I met at the Hollywood Christian Group. This began a situation that was one of my most unhappy times in my life.

Steve was a tall man of about forty. He was nothing spectacular, just someone to rescue me once in a while from the sadness of home responsibilities. Steve was a farm boy from North Dakota. He seemed enthralled when we started dating and admitted that he'd been watching me at some of the meetings of the Hollywood Group. He was in a high ecstasy of bliss. We talked by phone off and on during the day and most of the night. His enthusiasm was sweet, flattering, and infectious.

Steve had a small home on an acre of ground that he called Gopher Gulch. He owned his own business that he operated from his home. He was going through a divorce after his wife walked out on him.

I let him know from the start that I was not, at this point, marriage minded, but only going along for friendship. We were having a lot of fun together and he was fun to talk with. He had a fair amount of intelligence and we had fun swapping thoughts and views.

Our happy times of dating were short lived, because my parents took an exceptional dislike of him. It wasn't long before a nightmare situation developed in our household. Mom and Dad felt he was rude and disrespectful of them and had it firmly set in their minds that he wanted to take me over, get my home, and run them out in their old age.

I'd never had such an experience with my parents. My home had been my happy haven. I'd always had freedom. Mom had generally welcomed my choice of dates and half courted them herself. It was an outlet for her.

I attribute the change in Mom's attitude to her stroke and bad health. Also, she was afraid of losing me and being alone and stranded without a home. However, the behavior I saw in my parents was a type of hell that I'd never experienced in my life and it was my first time to even have a spirit of rebellion against their treatment.

Mom and Dad began treating me like a teenager and here I was over forty. They hounded me around the house and said that Steve must not come or phone. When we had a date, I would have to meet him at the curb. I must be in the house by midnight. It made them sick from worry. Mom would be crying when I left, and when I returned, the lights would be on and Dad would be walking the floor, while Mom was all laid out in distress over some gruesome session she had mentally or emotionally worked herself into.

I immediately tried calming her. I was sick at heart at how they were behaving. I felt trapped, my freedom was gone and there was no peace or happiness left for me, only a dead weight of unsolvable burden. What was I to do without some bit of outlet and relief from it all? At times, I felt I would crack up. The contact upheavals, pressure, and emotional strain that was brought to bear on me was breaking me down, and I was becoming ill. If Mom wasn't on me, she had Dad all torn up and yelling at me.

I assured them I wasn't going to marry Steve. He was just a friend. Dad would come back with, "Yeah, but he thinks you're going to marry him." I couldn't win.

I'd wait until they took their afternoon naps, then call Steve and ask him to come and pick me up at the curb. I'd take my bathing suit to sunbathe or a change of clothes if we went out to dinner. We often cooked dinner at his house. We'd just get comfortable by the fire when Mom would phone and badger me to come home.

For years, I'd always gone everywhere with my parents because I didn't drive. They would drop me off and pick me up later. I finally got a little Cadillac that was easy to handle and learned to drive. That was a major step toward my independence.

I would leave the house for a short while, even if it was to drive up into a nearby canyon road, where I would sit, play the radio, and feel some sense of freedom.

Poor Steve was helpless at understanding my parent's attitude toward him. He had compassion for my hemmed-in and ruled-over position. It finally became so unbearable that I had to hide from and avoid them in my home. I couldn't fight any longer. I got to the point where I was whipped down and had to surrender. There was no way we could live apart. I could hardly support us under one roof. I realized I had to make a complete break from Steve. So, I told him we had too many strikes against us to keep up the struggle. I suggested that we continue just as friends and have a mutual understanding when we saw each other at the Hollywood Group meetings. He seemed to understand.

So, I was back in the lap of family, alone and dateless, and a bit resentful.

CHAPTER 30 | Losing my Rock of Gibraltar

I tried to extricate myself from the possessiveness that had grown through the years with the three of us always being together. I tried to get Mom and Dad to go places without me. Mom, however, relied totally on me for her companionship. Everything I would try to plan for them became an issue. If I left the house, she would feel hurt and left out.

Mom, it was clear to see, was out of balance mentally, physically, and spiritually. Dad and I could sense that a crack-up was coming. Her outbursts were too numerous and frightening. It seemed to be building in her.

Then, suddenly, it came — another stroke. It was a bad one this time. Mom was rushed to the hospital under oxygen. The doctor thought maybe thinning her blood might help. After awhile, we couldn't keep up the expense of hospital care. We brought her home, rented a hospital bed, ordered oxygen tanks, and set up my doctor/nurse duties around the clock. There was simply no way we could afford hired nursing care.

I rarely got 10 or 15 minutes in my room before being called to duty. Dad and I traded nights staying on the sofa in her room. I administered certain shots to knock her out of her horrible suffering or I'd adjust the oxygen mask to correct the flow of oxygen to her lungs. Every responsibility was mine. Even the doctor began saying, "There's nothing I could do if I came, Joyce."

I became a walking, dragging zombie, trying to help Mom and shield Dad from too much stress, as he was about ready to keel over. We were at the point where any of us could drop dead, and one didn't know which would be first.

I'd sit on the side of her bed and look into her tortured brown eyes. She said, "I've always had hope, now I have none." She hated to leave, I know. Even more than going to be with the Lord, she had rather stay with me. I'm sure she felt I would never make it on my own.

If there were peaceful moments, I would try and comfort her about the inevitable. I'd say, "Grandma, Aunt Eula, Uncle Alvin, and Uncle Ray will be there. They will be waiting to greet you. She would think about it a little and look off in the distance as if trying to imagine and believe it. "I wonder," she replied.

One morning, I had dozed off a short time in my room. I awoke to the sound of her voice in a different moaning. I hurried to her. It was as if she was trying to say something, but couldn't. As she moaned and struggled, she looked at the ceiling with a dazed, pleading look in her eyes as she moaned and struggled. I realized her condition had gone into another phase, and she no doubt had had another stroke that had taken her speech.

Mom had been in this drastic state for three long months. This stroke must mean that the end was near. She would drift in and out of a coma and we would work over her body and try to make her comfortable. It was as if she were already gone.

Knowing her time was near, I left Dad to check on Mom while I went out alone and visited various funeral homes to check on casket prices and to make the arrangements. We didn't even have a burial plot. In checking one of the places, I found plots for a reasonable amount. So I bought two with my crumbs of money. One plot was for Mom, the other for Dad, when his time came.

The only casket I could possibly afford was a wooden box with metal handles. I went to a cloth shop and bought a few yards of taffeta to be arranged inside the casket. I bought the cloth home and made a little pillow to go under Mom's head. I laid out one of her pretty silk dresses she made. I sketched a picture of how I had kept her hair dressed, so the funeral home would know how to arrange her.

One, two, three days and nights came and went. I would think, as I sat by her bed wrapped in a blanket, that any minute now, the Lord would come and release her. I didn't want her to go out alone without me being by her side.

By the third day, I thought I couldn't stand it any longer. It was noon. I went to see Dad for a few minutes and came back with a desperate feeling in my heart. I had to do something. This couldn't go on another night.

I stepped up to the bed and stood at the back of her head and put my hands on either side of her face. I let out my heart-poured agony of prayer, "Father God, please, please release the spirit from this broken body."

At that second, the labored breathing stopped. The rise and fall of her chest ceased. It was so sudden, I gasped and stepped back. At last, her precious spirit had made its escape from her prison of flesh. Mom was free!

I went to her side, sat on the bed, and looked at what was left, the body I had handled and cared for so long. For the first time, my tears were set free to come. I let them flow, as I looked into the face of the one I had loved the most in my life and, I'm sure, the one who truly loved me the most.

I touched her dear face and eyelids, then bathed her face. I got a cloth and wrapped it under her chin and tied it atop her head so her face wouldn't fall before the funeral home came for her.

I went downstairs and told Dad that it was over. He came in weeping to see our beloved wife and mother. She was only 68 years old. I phoned the funeral home to come for her. I gave them the dress, pillow, and taffeta. I turned and realized it was all over. There was nothing left but an empty bed in Mom's room.

It was a warm and beautiful funeral service. Dad and I didn't sit in a family room behind drapes. He knelt a moment by her casket. Mom looked so pretty. I hadn't seen her so beautiful for such a long time. I had the huge casket bouquet arrangement in roses and a little wreath of pink carnations near her head. And her head rested on my pink pillow.

CHAPTER 31 | # My Attempt at Every Day Work

Dad and I were now alone. The heavy duties were over. It took a good year for Dad and me to regain our strength. I tried to pick Dad up from his shock, sadness, and depression. I took him everywhere with me. I planned social events for him, had groups of friends for luncheons, and took him to visit other friends. He decided he liked it and pulled out of the doldrums. He would say something like, "Well, have you got anything planned for us orphans today?"

Everyone liked Dad. He had a cute sense of humor and was a good story-teller and conversationalist.

Now that I was free again, I began to try my luck in the work-a-day world. We were so low in money. There were not enough studio calls to keep us in bread and butter, yet I had no other training but motion pictures.

I first decided to clean Mom's room and try to rent and share our home for a bit of quick income.

A nice couple who owned a flower shop came to live with us. They helped heal our loneliness that first Christmas after Mom was gone. They decorated the house with a Christmas tree downstairs and a small one upstairs for Dad and me. They loved the house and the big fireplace, where they'd sit in front of the fire and eat their meals on trays. They also liked to entertain, so Dad and I would give them privacy and stay in our rooms when they had company.

Meanwhile, I looked in the ads for work I might be able to do. My first under-taking was as an assistant to a manager of a furniture and appliance store. He had me selling, bookkeeping, and running to the bank. In between it all, he was chasing me around the furniture.

The store belonged to a lady who was home with a new baby and not around to keep tabs on what was going on. This guy was stealing her blind, and soon, the store and business were on the skids and about to go under. In a few months, it did! I was again looking for work.

Next, I answered an ad placed by a couple in the cosmetics business who needed help in their salon. The couple was selling their own line of cosmetics. The woman worked in someone else's beauty salon, while her husband made and packaged the cosmetics. They had a nice little salon in Beverly Hills and no one to run it, so they put me there. Of course, at the time, I didn't know that they were running out of money and about to go under.

I was to invite everyone I knew to come in for a free makeover and consul-tation. Then, I'd try to sell them a line of cosmetics. I was to be paid $50 each week, plus a commission of the sales.

I called all my friends and gave them soothing facials. They looked so good when I got through that they all bought the makeup. So far, so good! I eventu-ally found out, however, that I was out there on my own. I was on my feet all day and knocking myself out for the $50 a week. The problem was, I wasn't getting any commission. The couple began giving me some runaround. After awhile, they said they were closing the shop. I took up the commission issue with them. They gave me nothing. I decided to go to the labor board and get my few dollars.

I kept track of all I had sold, but they had all the sales receipts. They could show the labor board only the slips they chose. I was awarded the sum of $18.

My next job was to sell courses for a charm and modeling school. Since I had been in films, the owner wanted to advertise and use my name to publicize and sell a line of cosmetics he had. I was also to demonstrate and show customers how to properly apply makeup.

I didn't know his business circumstances until after getting into the job. He, too, had troubles. There was not enough business selling only the courses. The school was soon on the skids. The owner figured there was no reason to hang around, so he left for Las Vegas and played around out there.

The other girls working there, without supervision, soon played out and disappeared. Joycie wound up with the keys to the place. I had the responsibility of opening and closing the business, and in between, answering the phone and trying to sell courses. Finally, the owner showed up and shut down the place.

All of this was so ridiculous. There didn't seem to be a way for me to make a living out in the world.

I had done some nice oil paintings and had been practicing portrait work. I saw an empty store in Beverly Hills and inquired about renting the window at a reasonable price. I set up easels and arranged my wares. I printed place cards saying, "Oil paintings done for $25." No nibbles! So, I closed my own business.

Dad had a small old age pension, but with food, utilities, gas for the car, and property taxes, it wasn't enough to get us by. We struggled on.

CHAPTER 32

My Fling with a Gay Minister

Here and there, I'd find someone to date, but I usually ended up having to discard them for one reason or another. I continued going to the Hollywood Christian Group. They were my lifeline.

It was at a meeting of this group that I met a very attractive young minister in his early forties. He took note of me and soon arranged for some friends of mine to plan a date for us to go out together. Richard was an associate pastor at one of our big churches and he also taught some single's classes there.

He was a whiz at what he did and was quite popular. Some of the girls had problem crushes on him. He didn't seem to get involved with anyone; he was just nice to everyone.

I was rather pleased with his attention of me and he asked me to all their church social functions. We certainly looked good together. He was at the right age, had never married, was well educated, and had an interesting personality. I thought maybe I'd found something special.

Richard was totally fascinated by my film background and was always looking at my glamour photos. He would often bring someone to the house to meet me and to look at the movie stuff. He wasn't narrow or condemning as some ministers had been.

Richard would say things like, "Joycie, the movie star," and other cute and complimentary things. He greeted me with a little peck on the cheek and the same when he left. He was proud to show me off. Now and then, I went to some premiere or a special showing of a film and would ask him to escort me.

There was no serious intimacy, which was alright by me, but after things seemed to be taking a more serious tone and turn, I wanted to be a bit closer. I was rather frustrated. I thought maybe he was who I had been waiting for all these years. He was also the first one of any consequence I'd dated since Mom left us.

Richard had a little apartment and pool across from the church. Sometimes, when he was so busy on the weekends, I'd fix some food, take my swimsuit, and drive down to be with him. I knew a lot of the youngsters at his church and they would come to his apartment and swim in the pool. There was always some activity going on.

On one occasion, he would mention a niece that he had been brought up with and was very fond of and close to. She was married, had a small child, and lived back in their hometown. I heard she often left her family at Christmas to come and spend the holidays with her Uncle Richard. On other occasions, she would make trips to where he happened to be holding meetings. I would say things like, "If I didn't know she was your niece, I might be jealous."

Then, out of nowhere, Richard wrote a letter asking me to marry him. He wanted my answer the next time he came to see me. We were to spend an evening, alone for a change, at my house. I was really geared for something warm and closer between us, after some months of staying at bay in affection.

The evening came. I indicated my willingness to share his life and work. Then, I made myself available in little ways to at least have some meaningful kissing to seal the deal. To not be affectionate and pop into a marriage cold turkey would be a rather strange and embarrassing situation. I never had to seek affection, but usually ended up having to fight it off on occasion.

Suddenly, almost without warning, Richard moved away from me and said he had to leave. I was stunned. He was acting like a shy and frightened girl. Something must be wrong at the point of affection. I was dumbfounded.

We stopped talking marriage, but continued to go together to social events. He usually came to pick me up with another person, and he and the other person would usually take me home. He'd give me the usual peck on the cheek.

Then, he told me his niece was coming to town for a visit. He wanted me to come down to the apartment and go with him to meet her at the airport. So, I joined him there, or, I should say, I joined them there, as he had a young fellow at the apartment with him. As it happened, the plane was late arriving. There were multiple delays, so all three of us ended up waiting there and napping until almost daylight. How inconvenient for me!

We met the plane and I met the niece. She was young and quite pretty, and you have never seen such an elated uncle. He was a different fellow around her. Every look, every attention was on her.

The apartment had only one bedroom with twin beds. People at the church offered her a place to stay, but she and the uncle had always slept in the same room while growing up, so why change now? They needed to talk, be together, and on and on.

I went back to the apartment and got acquainted with her. I finally opened up and talked frankly about Richard. She indicated that she and the rest of the family at home were expecting us to marry. I told her that there was some strange side of him concerning affection and that I thought perhaps he had a fear or insecurity about women. She squirmed a bit, but defended her uncle, again saying the family expected us to marry.

Regardless of what she said, I knew something wasn't right with him. Richard was a different person around her. I was practically non-existent. He walked close to her arm-in-arm, leaving me to trail along ignored. I was mystified.

Sometime after, I was at the home of some friends and brought up the subject of Richard and his strange behavior. "This man is a homosexual," they informed a stunned Joycie. "If you had married this man, he would have used you as a front for his ministry and you would have wound up in the backseat of the car."

I was flabbergasted and doubted what they said — at first! Then, I began to look back at things and remember the times Richard had brought handsome, young fellows with him to pick me up for dates. Or, he would pick someone up at a dinner or party and offer them a ride home. They'd dropped me off and away they'd go. I remembered the times at the beach when he would strike up a quick acquaintance and invite some fellow home with him.

I had thought nothing about it. The fellows were clean cut and innocent looking young men. I even warned him of picking up strangers and inviting them to stay with him. He'd brush it off and insist he was befriending and showing someone on leave from the service a good time.

How could I have been so naïve and innocent after having been in Hollywood so long? I never confronted Richard or said anything to him about us. It was just the way things were with him. I forgot it and thanked my lucky stars I'd escaped a horrible experience.

As things turned out, we often crossed paths through the years. He would always turn up with a phone call and tell me what he was doing or where he had moved. He'd ask, "How's the movie star?" He always enjoyed what I had to say, would laugh, and reply, "Joyce, you're so funny." I think he knew that I knew about him, but we said nothing.

Richard would meet and date some little picture actress — he liked to have women friends — and most of the girls would be smitten by his charm. The last time I heard from him, he was in Las Vegas or Reno performing wedding ceremonies.

CHAPTER 33 | *I Tie the Knot, or Does it Tie Me?*

After my frustrating experience with the gay minister, I needed to get far away from Hollywood and enjoy a change of scenery. It seemed I'd now experienced about every reason as to why I shouldn't marry.

The change I needed came when I took a trip to Twin Lakes in the High Sierras with my friends, Elisa and Jim. We drove all night getting to the mountains so we wouldn't be going through the hot desert in the day. Elisa and Jim's son, Edgar, also came with us. Edgar, a teenager, was a handsome lad, but he and his father were so incompatible. As they went off trout fishing every day, I fully expected one to come home in the evening saying one had killed the other.

Poor Elisa had to be the go-between in the heated arguments and dissention. I honestly don't know how she lived through the turmoil in their lives. She and Jim also had their disagreements. This quarrelsome atmosphere wasn't pleasant to be in, and I'd stay apart as much as I could.

With the fellas away everyday on their fishing and sporting jaunts, I was sort of a companion for Elisa. She had been a movie and stage star in Hungary when she met and married Jim, thinking he had more wealth than he had.

Elisa and I would pack our lunch and take the boat and paddle around or float lazily on the lake. We might sunbathe or drift into the shade and talk the afternoon away.

We had been there about a week and, with a Sunday coming up, we decided to attend church at an outdoor chapel near the Tamorack Lodge.

As we walked the road to our destination, there was a most attractive car and small sleeping trailer. The owner was just arriving to settle in the campground area. It was a brand new Chrysler, sort of mustard color, and the trailer was painted to match.

When the church service was over, we headed back to the road to walk towards our cabin. As we were walking along, we became conscious of a fellow and his cocker spaniel catching up with us. We met and spoke casually as one does at a resort. We continued walking together towards the campground until we reached our cabin.

He said his name was Bill and that he was there for a week or so on his vacation. In the course of conversation, he invited Elisa and me to come to his trailer in the afternoon for a visit. We accepted. He picked us up, and, would you believe, his car was that new Chrysler and trailer I had commented on earlier?

Bill was quite interesting and a good conversationalist. His eyes were blue, his teeth were white, and he just sparkled with wholesomeness. We couldn't tell which one of us he might be interested in. Later, he said that he liked what he saw — *me!* He'd had his eye on me the moment he arrived at the campground and deliberately managed to meet us on the trail. So, fate was taking place.

Bill lost no time in asking to see me again and since he was to be there on vacation, he asked me out. We had picnics during the day and dinner every evening at various spots around the campground. Things moved along — fast!

Elisa and Jim were somewhat put out with me, because my dating left Elisa alone during the day, and every evening, I was out with Bill until midnight. "Why did she come, if she wanted to stay out nightclubbing?" Jim asked.

Bill's vacation days rolled by and we crammed in every moment of our fast-moving relationship. We wasted no time in getting acquainted and swapping our life histories. If we had been in town, it would have taken us several months to find out this much about the other.

Bill was 46 and had been married twice before. Bill's work was in Long Beach, as was his small frame house he had lived in with his last wife. He seemed to have some hold over for the last one and kept saying that I reminded him of her. I brushed it aside and was more interested in how we were feeling about each other. Bill seemed really sweet and was comfortable to be with, sort of housebroken.

As I look back in it, I realize I threw caution to the wind. I just wanted to get on with things and see what there was between us. I was fed up with all my disastrous experiences and coming to the conclusion that no one would ever be perfect. I would have to take a chance on someone or risk spending my life alone.

Bill's vacation came to an end and he left for Los Angeles. I stayed on with my friends a couple of more weeks. After so much time together, I really missed Bill. I was interested to see what would happen when I returned home. There would be another side to us, our home turf. We would have to determine how we felt about each other and how we stacked up.

Back home, we looked forward to our first meeting. Right from the start, things continued on a serious note. Bill would come to my house for a weekend with Dad and me. Then, I'd take some clothes and go back with him to stay a few days. We talked, discussed, and planned.

On one of those weekends, we decided we wanted to marry. Dad was supportive. He said, "I won't be here forever, and if you feel you've found someone you can get along with and care about, you have my blessings." That was all I needed to hear. He wasn't going to be a problem or stand in the way of my freedom. This would have been impossible had Mom still been alive. If she hadn't had a stroke, she surely would have had one over this.

I convinced Bill to make our living quarters in my home. There was so much room for us there and building that house had been one of my most cherished accomplishments. He would rent his home in Long Beach and transfer his work to a nearby branch of the jewelry company where he'd worked for years.

Bill balked at the thoughts of Dad being in the house with us. I talked to Dad saying, "Run for your life. Let us have some privacy. Don't butt in. Let Bill be the boss." I told Dad to have his dinner before Bill got home and to be in his room with his TV and interests. Dad and Bill agreed to these terms.

On one trip to see me, Bill had a lovely three-carat diamond ring to put on my finger. We also had wedding bands for each other. Mine had eight small diamonds. I told Bill I wanted only one ornament, a little diamond cross.

In years past, I'd seen and kept a picture of the wedding dress I wanted if I ever took that step. I bought the material and worked on it between dates with Bill. I didn't want white, as I, being 48 years old, was not a young bride. I chose a very pale shade of pink.

I also made all the arrangements, from making and mailing invitations, to planning the reception at the church, gathering ushers, selecting hostesses, and on and on. I had to attend to it all. I had no one to do anything for me at any time, it seemed. I was very tired, but tried to keep all aglow with Bill.

The courtship had been a little less than my usual three-month inspection of a person I was going with. I took the final steps toward marriage.

Bill was a bit strange at times. He seemed to be getting the jitters, I'm sure, but his attitude was definitely knocking the bloom off things. I didn't quite know what to expect from him. He could be so warm, sweet, and giving. Then, another side of him would creep through that seemed cold, hard, and calculating. This didn't give me a good feeling of security, by any means.

At some point, for example, he said he would have his attorney draw up an agreement for us to sign for our own protection. Protection from what, I wondered? He wasn't a moneyed person, and I certainly had no notion of wanting anything material from him. He gave the papers to me one evening, but I refused to look them over until the next day. It was a type of protection that Bill could walk off and drop me at anytime.

His insistence on the agreement put a damper on my feelings. What attitudes to start a marriage with, I thought. I signed the document, but decided at the last minute to take it to an attorney for another opinion. The attorney said to tear off my signature and return the agreement.

Time was narrowing down. The eve of the wedding rehearsal had arrived. The wedding was scheduled for the following evening at 8 p.m. at Hollywood Presbyterian Church.

Bill called and said he and his party were coming in from Long Beach for the rehearsal. We headed to the church. The rehearsal went on with all our instructions. As Bill was getting ready to drive back to Long Beach with his friends, he asked for the papers. I handed it to him. "I've seen an attorney and have been advised not to sign this," I said. "We can't have a marriage with such an agreement. I hope you don't mind."

Bill turned white, and, as cold as steel, said, "I do mind!" The wedding party was waiting for him, so there was no time to discuss my refusal to sign the paper. I knew there was trouble ahead, and at the eleventh hour!

He called as soon as he got home, but I refused to answer. I couldn't face a harangue on the phone for hours, perhaps all night. What an awful night it was.

At the crack of dawn, the day of my wedding, Bill was on my doorstep to have it out. He was a wild man. He said he wasn't about to marry without a signed agreement. The more he demanded, the more I stood my ground. He reminded me of his two failed marriages and said he was judging me by his thinking and experiences. We were in a deadlock and about to cancel the whole thing.

I told Dad we were about to have a miscarriage of a marriage. He suggested we talk with the minister who was to marry us. When Bill and I sat in front of the minister and told him what was going on, he said he couldn't perform the ceremony if such an agreement was in effect, that the union would not be a marriage. He tried to talk sense into Bill.

Bill and I were drained at this point. I was numb! We drove up one of the canyons near my house and climbed up a hill. We sat there together and discerned what direction we take. Finally, Bill said, "Well, we can't be married with an agreement. If you will verbally swear there would be no trouble if things don't work out, I'll accept that." I agreed.

The evening of our wedding arrived. What should have been one of the happiest days of my life started as one of the worst. I felt dead inside. Nothing seemed real. I was going through movie scenes playing my role. Everyone was fussing over their appearances while totally ignoring me. No one helped or even looked at me, as I got into my beautiful dress. It really wasn't my show, but just a movie scene. It wasn't my wedding dress, but a costume. The director would soon say, "Lights, camera, action," and I would walk into the set and play my role.

Finally, it was over. Bill and I left together. Dad went on home. There was no dinner party planned for us afterwards. We drove to a drive-in hamburger stand near my home. Sitting there in my puffy wedding dress, we ate hamburgers alone. Was this how it was supposed to be?

We drove to my home. Two of my friends were waiting to see us and present us their gifts. We visited a bit and opened some of the presents.

After our friends left, I went upstairs to undress. It was late and all were weary. Bill said he was going to take the dog for a walk.

I'd given him Mom's room to store his things. I put on my pretty silk robe and gown I'd made and crawled into my antique sleigh bed. I waited and waited! What had happened to Bill on our wedding night? Had he gotten lost in the area?

After several hours, he came in. I didn't rush to say anything. I just waited. He came up the steps. My door was open, the lights were on. I thought he would surely come in and say something about where he had been and offer some explanation. He didn't!

He got undressed and crawled into bed in Mom's room.

Dear God, I thought, what kind of a man have I married?

He certainly wasn't going to make a move, so I went and asked him what was wrong.

"I'm sick," he replied.

"You want some baking soda?" I asked.

"No," he answered, "it's this house."

Bill had himself worked up over thinking about living here and not having pride of ownership. I realized I had a baby on my hands, not a man, not a lover, not a husband, not even a person who loved me, as far as I could see. I figured I would have to make the best of a bad situation and a coax a nut out of his pouting, fearful doldrums.

"Why don't you want to come on over and be with me?" I asked. "We'll talk all of this over tomorrow."

He allowed himself to be drawn into my bed, where we slept like two sticks. I saw to it, however, that the next morning, the marriage was consummated.

We left for Lake Arrowhead on our honeymoon. Some friends of mine had set us up in their place. I didn't want the honeymoon to be wasted on a stranger. At the rate things were going, I was beginning to think I might as well have married the gay minister.

I drove all the way to the mountains. Driving was an outlet for me, after all the tension I'd felt. Since we'd have a place to cook, I thought we'd have some fun playing house and cooking our meals. We stopped at a market to pick up some groceries to take up. While shopping, I picked up a candy bar and looked at the price. It was about 15¢ or so. Bill exclaimed, "Oh, do you want this?" I could see the price disturbed him.

"Never mind," I answered. "Forget it."

"Well, if you really want it," he said, as he tossed it back.

I was embarrassed in front of the checker. I was experiencing another point in Bill's makeup. He was cheap.

Bill had brought along a nice movie camera. He said his ex-wife had no idea what to do in front of a camera. He was so excited to have someone who could plan things to do on film, give some action, and plan some cute scenes.

We were settling in and sort of back to the original setting in which we'd first met. It was like putting all our problems aside that had arisen between us and abandoning ourselves to relive our first days.

Bill could be affectionate, warm, and giving. Our lovemaking was good and fulfilling. After all, he'd had many years of experience.

During the days, we took a boat out to an island in the lake. I took a bathing suit and some lingerie. I'd plan scenes and action for our movies. I'd play the scene completely unconscious of the camera. Like a kid, unaware. I'd look this way and that, step behind a bush, and come out with another change of panties or whatever. Then, I'd run to the water's edge and dabble a foot in the cold water like a Sennett bathing beauty.

Back at our playhouse every evening, I'd really plan productions. What fun! I got to be the star and have all the close-ups I wanted. I turned loose with complete abandon and felt a sense of freedom I'd never known. Away from my family, I finally felt I had a life of my own.

We had all our home movies to look forward to when we got home. The films were a record of what I hoped for our future.

We were soon back home to have our try at marriage and sort of pick up where we left off with Bill's attitudes. The honeymoon was behind us.

Bill seemed to harbor hatred for my dad, and from Bill's comments, the reason became evident to me. He was jealous of my home, because it wasn't his. He resented all the things Dad had done and accomplished with it. Bill would say, "I have no pride of ownership," or "It may be in your name, but it's still more your dad's."

Dad gave way for Bill to be the head of the household and stayed away from us when Bill was home.

I gave a lovely dinner party and invited some of the neighbors, so that Bill would feel part of the community. He put our film together and played it for the party. Bill began to pick on me with little petty and snide remarks, such as, "You photograph better than you look." I agreed, but added, "I didn't expect you to tell me so." He would pick on my manner of speech, saying, "You speak so indistinctly that my friends cannot understand what you are saying." I replied that, yes, with my bit of a Southern accent, I do slur my words.

I finally said, "Isn't it strange, Bill, how perfect we were before marriage and how imperfect we are after?"

We were in my house about a week or two. Bill hadn't transferred his work here, but still commuted to Long Beach. He stopped coming home, preferring to stay over at his Long Beach house. This went on for about two weeks.

The next time he came over, I saw the familiar papers under his arm, the agreements he had his attorney draw up for us to sign. He let me know he wasn't coming back here to live.

I turned the tables when I told him that I would pack a few clothes and return with him to his small house. I came up to my room and cried out, "Dear God, what have I done to deserve this?" All I wanted was a little happiness of my own.

Our wedding gifts were still in the living room. As we were getting ready to leave, Bill said, "Let's take some things with us." I was hurrying to get things in the car. When we were leaving, I saw Bill had taken the gifts his friends had given. He said he was just showing me he wasn't coming back.

As we turned the street corner and pulled out of the neighborhood, I have never felt such a depth of sorrow, not even at Mom's passing. I felt my heart and soul were being torn out as I left the home I'd worked so hard for.

We made the trip mostly in silence. As we reached his house, I ran in and threw myself across the bed and gave release to sobbing.

For a while, I was suffocated with my grief. I finally realized that unless I changed my attitude, I was going to be very sick and could never cope with any of this. I picked up the pieces of our rocky start and began my role playing. I took an interest in my limited surroundings and tried to figure what I could do with it.

It seemed his house had no room for me, no space for the bit of clothing I'd brought, much less any real possessions.

Sometimes, it all seemed so ridiculous that I had gotten myself into such a predicament that I'd just start laughing. His dog would crawl out from under the furniture and look at me as if to say, "What is so funny?"

Occasionally, I would drive home when I had to attend to something for my abandoned Dad. He had never been alone before. Now, at his age, everyone was gone. He said that at first, he thought he would lose his mind. Then, like me, he realized he had to get hold of himself. He started to have his own little dinner parties for a couple of friends.

Now and then, I probably looked troubled and downcast in the predicament I was struggling with. Bill was on the lookout to see if he could step in and make a deal with me about my home. I knew he would offer to help me pay the taxes if I would put his name on my property. I was also aware that if I ever sold or made some change, he would make his demands and get his share.

He would say, "You need to get out and work and I'll stay home for a change." He was jealous that I wasn't out earning my share of the groceries. He gave me a small amount for our food twice a month. There was nothing for anything I might need and I really didn't want anything. He couldn't have had a more reasonable girl to clean, cook, do the laundry, market, take his clothes to the cleaners, bed with him in that tiny room, and share his dog and its fleas. All he was out on me was my food, and I thought I earned that!

Every evening, the dog and I would watch for Bill. I'd say, "Here comes daddy," and we would run to greet her. Bill would come in and head straight for the dog, leaving me standing alone. I'd say, "Bill you love that dog more than you do me." He'd reply, "When I've known you as long as I've known Rosie, maybe I'll love you that much."

Now and then, he reeked of cigarettes, but I knew that Bill didn't smoke! So, I figured he had his old girlfriend, who worked at a nearby health food store, to drop him off at home. I suspected she had kissed him goodbye and left her smell on his breath and clothes. I also knew he went to lunch with his ex-wife. He was void of affection and would comment, "I will probably never love anyone again as I did my wife." He would even ask if I didn't feel her presence in the house.

I concluded that Bill had married me to comfort the hurt of losing the wife he loved. He was getting even with her by showing her that he had replaced her with a film actress. Then, I feel he was obsessed with benefiting himself materially, either through my home or my work. When not berating me, he would say how well I photographed when we made our films, and that "if you took these films to the studios, they might give you a big contract."

One day, I drove home to take care of some business. Because of a heavy rainstorm, I stayed with Dad most of the week. Bill and I didn't talk the whole time I was away. When I returned, I saw evidence that there had been two staying at the house.

When he came in from work, I expect we both knew in our hearts that this was it. In the course of events, we discussed our situation and were in agreement that things would be better if we parted.

"Now you see, Bill," I said, "It is over and there will be no trouble. None of those things you feared, those obsessions that spoiled our life together, will come to pass."

We even stirred up a last romantic parting between us and there were a few words of sentiment for what might have been. The extent of our happiness consisted only of the one week of abandoned honeymooning at Lake Arrowhead.

I got my clothes together and collected a few pots and pans I had brought with me. The poor man never knew where to quit. I laid my set of car and house keys on the table and he offered me a $50 check, explaining this is what remained in a small checking account after his attorney and court costs were paid. The $50 was my share!

"Bill, don't add insult to injury," I said as I threw the check on the table. "You don't owe me anything."

I guess he told his friends that he had given me a settlement. I told mine that I'd just finished a three-month, legal love affair!

Dad didn't know I was coming home. Bill and I walked in with all my pots and pans in arms. The house was all lit up, a big fire was roaring in the fireplace, and the dining room table was set. Dad was having a dinner party for his friends, and here I came, the prodigal. What a homecoming! It was like entering heaven after being in the lower regions.

Bill wept a little as he brought things in and told me I'd certainly done my part in this experience. As he walked out the door, he turned and, looking at all the warmth, beauty, and comfort, said, "This is where you belong. I never should have taken you out of it."

I realized, in our hectic three months of marriage, which seemed like half of an eternity, that physical relations are totally empty and meaningless without a love shared between the two people.

When it was over, I wept a little over my attempt to find a crumb of happiness of my own. Of course, I would never try marriage again. I allowed myself one mistake and this one was it!

CHAPTER 34 | *Finding my way after Bill*

In due time, I went to court. At first, the plan was to let Bill get a divorce. I was advised that this wasn't fair to me and left a bad record. So, a plan was made whereby I could have an annulment.

As for Bill, I heard later that he married his fourth wife, the woman he had dated at the health food store. I heard from a Long Beach acquaintance that this marriage also failed. Surprised?

With Bill behind me, I had to pick myself up and find a source of livelihood. Renting Mom's room and sharing my house was the fastest approach to a bit of income. Dad contributed $40 each month from his small pension.

I had some dribbles of television work once in a blue moon, shows such as *Richard Diamond, Private Detective; The Adventures of Jim Bowie;* and *Pete and Gladys.* One of my final film roles was in *Girl in the Woods* in the late 1950s. These jobs, one or two days of work, equated to peanut pay. I had a few extra crumbs through residuals after a television job. I did a Christian film for Bob Pearce of Samaritan's Purse, a missionary ministry.

I also searched the ads and saw a job I thought I could handle. The Broadway department store on Hollywood Boulevard wanted someone to demonstrate paint-by-number sets over the Christmas holidays. I took some of my paintings to show them and had no trouble getting the job. It was not the type of art work that I sought, but it would only be a couple of weeks' employment.

There I was on Hollywood Boulevard, doing my thing. They put me on the main floor with a table full of paint sets to sell and a place to sit and demonstrate how to paint by numbers. I didn't mind. I liked to paint and I could meet the public with no problems. I had no problem getting people interested in trying their hand at painting. I sold sets faster than they kept me supplied and would dart off to their stock room to replace the sets that people bought. My boss at Broadway said they had never had a painter who promoted sales as I had. They were quite pleased and complimentary; however, there was no commission, only the small weekly check.

Dad drove me to work and picked me up every evening. Two nights a week, I worked until 9 p.m. By the end of those shifts, I was weary and my eyes were strained. People would come by and recognize me from films and wonder what I was doing there. Who cared? They were not paying my bills.

When the holidays were over, so was my job. I tried several other things. Someone told me that if I went to an agency and signed up for childcare, I could get a rate of $1 an hour. I thought I could do this, although I'd never been around children or handled an infant. It wouldn't be out in the public, and I'd not have to answer questions about why I, a movie actress, was doing public work.

In filling out the application, I saw questions about nursing. Bingo! I was surely qualified in most areas of practical and private duty nursing at home with patients. This job paid a rate of $2 an hour. They would want care for eight hours a day and maybe for several days or a few weeks. I could see that the care I gave Mom was invaluable and Mom's doctors thought I was a great nurse. I was on my way to a new career.

After I got going with the agency calls, I signed with several patients. They had good reports about me and began recommending me to others. I told my doctors what I was doing, and it wasn't long before they would call me to sit with their patients who were being released from the hospital.

When calls came in, I'd don my white nursing uniform, grab my nursing case, and be off across the Valley to the aid of ailing humanity.

Each case was different and called for different skills, although one skill was constant — compassion. I compared each case to taking on a new film job, playing a new role for each case. However, these were real-life roles and I was playing them to the hilt.

It was an experience for me to handle newborn babies, to prune, polish, and powder them, while being careful not to throw them out with the bath water. Often the mother and family would stand by in awe at how deftly and confidently I handled these wee treasures they had brought into the world, yet were sometimes too afraid and timid to handle themselves.

Often, a new mother was sick herself and the other children needed to be cared for, not to mention the new infant and a husband coming home to face the whole thing. These types of situations called for me to be capable and efficient and to stretch my talents and energies in many directions.

I'd sometimes take over diets and plan and prepare proper foods. Some patients would revive and turn their sick systems around.

I got a phone call to rush to the aid of Aileen, a dear little lady who'd broken her ankle and was in a cast. She had gotten home from the hospital, couldn't manage her crutches, fell onto the floor, and dragged herself to the phone to call an agency for help.

We got along famously and I was with her awhile. She had a gift shop business and was widowed with no children.

Sometime later, a friend of Aileen's called to say that she had attempted suicide by taking a handful of pills. Aileen had called this friend to come the next morning to make sure she would be found and not lie dead in her apartment for days.

It seems that Aileen had been to an eye doctor who told her she was losing her eyesight. Being alone, not too young, and perhaps a bit lonely and depressed, she figured her prospects for a bright future were slim.

I was called in to pull the pieces together. She decided suicide was not the solution and promised not to try again. The pills only made her sick and the means they used to save her life were not pleasant.

After a few days with Aileen, she decided it would be good for her to get away. She asked me to drive her to Palm Springs for a week or so. Although she smoked like a fiend, I made the best of things and got Aileen around town for whatever she wanted to do. We took the mineral baths, swam in the hot pools, and ate at different places around town.

When we returned to Los Angeles, I helped her get settled into an apartment. She got better as time went on and was capable of living on her own.

My nursing career was turning into some of the most fulfilling work I'd ever done.

CHAPTER 35 | *Becoming an Orphan*

I became concerned about leaving Dad for very long at a time, as he seemed to be slipping mentally and acting rather strangely. We were fortunate that we had a renter, Ruth, who kept an eye on him when I was gone.

When I went out on my nursing calls, I would fix food and leave it for him, and call home to check on him during the day. Then, when I came home in the evening, he would have the doors bolted. I would call to him. He'd peep out or ask if anyone was with me. He looked strange in his eyes and seemed full of fear.

Dad thought someone was out to get him. He carried a pistol strapped under his arm during the day. He became suspicious of the neighbors and decided they were peddling dope.

I was in another quandary about what to do. He wouldn't hear of going to a doctor. He would often call our neighbor, Olive, to come over and talk with him. He would tell her what he thought was going on in the neighborhood. Then, he would tell me that he thought Olive looked strange and that she must be on dope. He said the same about me. I was concerned, but not sure what to do about his behavior.

I got a call from the studio for one day of work on *Pete and Gladys*, a television show. I picked up the script and was to go to work the next morning. That evening, Ruth's boyfriend came to see her and Dad invited the two into his bedroom to talk. He rambled from subject to subject, but it made sense. He didn't give anyone a chance to leave the room. I sat in the hall and watched through his cracked door. He wanted me to come in, too, but I told him I had to study my script.

Later, Ruth came in from her date and was in bed. Sometime in the night, I heard Dad raging and talking in his room. I knew there was trouble ahead. What was I to do? I knew better than to come out and go to his door, and I didn't want to call the police and start an episode in the dark of night. Dad would be so frightened and, in the mental state I knew he was in, he might shoot and harm anyone who got in his way.

I had to warn Ruth and get us both safely out of the house and keep her from going in the hall. Our closets joined our bedrooms and off and on I tried to tap on the wall to arouse and tell her the circumstances and make a plan. Dad had, in the past, raged throughout the night, and then got quiet before daylight.

I finally got Ruth awake and told her not to go in the hall until I had my plan made and gave the signal. I called Olive, our neighbor, and told her what was going on and that I was going to get Ruth and me out of the house. We would go to Olive's house. I would make up for my role at her house. Ruth would drive me to the studio, and I would send a friend to the house and see what we could do with Dad.

We opened our doors and hurried down the stairs and out the back way before Dad could catch us. He would be desperate and believe something was going to happen to him. His instinct would be to protect himself in whatever way possible.

Ruth and I made a dash for it. We escaped from the house and ran to Olive's, where we stayed the rest of the night. As I was getting made up to go to the studio, I heard the police at our house. Dad had gotten scared with Ruth and me gone. He shot a hole in the bedroom door and ceiling, and broke out a window. He was calling for help and brandishing his gun.

Everyone was out in the street and trying to coax Dad to come down and give up. I knew I would be late getting to the studio. The director said they would take other scenes until I got there.

The police finally got Dad to surrender and come out. What a nightmare it all was. I have no idea how I managed to remember my lines and do the day's work.

Dad was taken to the psychiatric ward at General Hospital in downtown Los Angeles. It was up to me to drive there on my own and attend to whatever was coming next. It was difficult for me to find my way downtown, find an area to park, and get to the hospital. When I did see him, he was so pitiful and looked so ill and helpless. He thought I had come to rescue him and take him home. I sat down beside him and put my arm around his frail shoulders and tried to comfort him.

Doctors and psychiatrists were going to run tests and see what was happening to him. I was told to return in 10 days to discuss what should be done. In the meantime, I went on another nursing case.

When I returned to the hospital 10 days later, I was told that Dad's blood to his brain was not circulating properly. He hallucinated and saw people all distorted. That's why he thought everybody he saw was doing drugs. I was urged to put him in a sanitarium.

The doctors advised me not to visit too often for fear of upsetting him. Sure enough, when I visited, he jumped up and down, thinking I'd come for him. He got on his knees and begged me to take him home. When he found out I had only come for a visit, he'd turn sullen and mean towards me. My visits would make me sick for days.

It was heart wrenching to think of the hard work he'd put into the house and the dedication he'd had to me and my career, only to be put away in an institution, away from both the house and me.

After Dad had been hospitalized for some time, our neighbor, Olive, who thought so much of Dad, encouraged me to bring Dad home and to give him a try at living in the real world. Out of the guilt Olive laid on me, I broke down and decided to bring Dad home.

His doctors advised me against the decision. However, I couldn't live with myself unless I gave Dad the chance he begged for. Also, if he stayed on his medication, he might be okay and have the chance to die in his own home.

I did everything possible to hold Dad together. I made sure he took his medication, prepared nutritious meals for him, and talked about the good times we'd had in the past. I left him while I went to work, but would call often to check on him. As time went on, I saw Dad become morose, sink into depression, and exhibit disturbing mood swings.

One morning, as I was leaving for work, I knocked on his door to tell him goodbye. I couldn't get an answer. I continued to knock until he opened the door. He staggered and fell back across the bed. Then, I saw. He had saved up his tranquilizers and had taken them in an attempt to end his life. Turns out, he never lost consciousness. I later found many pills scattered over the floor.

After this scare, I realized Dad needed to be in a place where he could receive constant attention. I called the institution where Dad had stayed, but they had no room for him. I called a neighbor to come and sit with him while I phoned various facilities.

While I was on the phone, I heard a scuffle downstairs. I ran down to find Dad and Tom wrestling on the floor. Dad had attacked him with a cane and was heading toward the back porch. By then, his strength had diminished and he tripped and fell. There he laid, so spent and pitiful, the fight all gone. I got a pillow for his head. Dad uttered, "Put me somewhere. I know I'm sick."

The police came, then an ambulance. Dad was taken to General Hospital downtown. This time, I knew more about Dad's condition. They said they would have to administer psychiatric evaluations and tests. Then, there would be a court trial and procedure for having Dad committed.

I thought they would send Dad to another closed sanatorium. Instead, they sent him to Camarillo State Mental Hospital. I just went to pieces, my tears streamed at the thought that we were throwing away my pitiful little Dad.

I didn't see Dad again until he was settled in Camarillo. I drove up to visit and to take him some clothes. When I saw Dad, he was in a straight jacket and restrained in bed. He wouldn't be needing clothes, they said. I could take them back.

It's a wonder I didn't lose my mind during all this. If Dad wasn't already in trouble, he surely was after all he had been through. After his sheltered life with Mom and me, he was being yanked out of his home into all the chaos that had become his life.

Shock treatments and medication helped Dad forget a lot of the pressures in his life: Mom's illness and death and my marriage. I once brought up my disastrous marriage.

His reply? "You were married?"

All those memories were gone.

I was free to carry on with my nursing work knowing Dad was safe and getting some type of care. I visited him every weekend, and there were times when I could bring him home for a week or so.

After over two years in the Camarillo State Hospital, Dad was given the clearance to leave the facility. I panicked. There was no way I could bring him home. I couldn't cope with it. I still had to make a living and there was no one at home to care for him. We were in no position to hire help. The facility finally got my message and agreed to put Dad in a residential-type setting in Ventura.

Dad was happy there and completely free. He was no longer locked up or strapped to the bed. He had his own private room and went to the dining room for his meals. I visited every weekend. I'd take him out in the car and we'd park along the beach. His speech became garbled and I had trouble understanding him, so we often just sat in silence. It gave him comfort just to have me there.

He was in this place for about a year. As time had gone on, I could see he was getting weaker. He would totter across the street into traffic. I looked around for other places that would be closer than Ventura. After some inquiries, I found a type of care facility that was housed in Guy Kibbee's big colonial home. A little hospital had been built on the property, so that if anything happened, the resident could be close to medical care.

With him being this close, I practically took over his care. I'd take clippers and trim his hair. I shaved and bathed him. I'd fix some good foods and take over for him and the other residents to enjoy. I'd put him in a wheelchair and race him around the block. He loved the pampering and I was happy I could do things for him.

One day, I was talking to him on the phone and he just disappeared. He'd suffered a heart attack, dropped the phone, and slumped forward. He was sent to the hospital. My little sweetheart Dad was never out again. He just kept fading and growing weaker. There seemed to be nothing left for him.

One Sunday morning, about three months after he'd moved to the facility, the hospital called to say that Dad just "slipped away." My sweet Dad, at 79 years old, had gone peacefully to sleep. He was set free, never to suffer again, never to be alone.

Our family threesome was over. I was now a total orphan. No kin left. I buried Dad at Mom's side in Valhalla Cemetery. Joycie came home to carry on once more. This time, I was quite alone.

It was good I still had my nursing job to keep me focused and occupied. Shortly after Dad passed, I took several trips. There were only two places I wanted to visit: Hawaii and my beloved Tulsa, where 40 years before, as a wild-eyed, star-struck teenager, I'd left to seek my fortune in Hollywood. It seemed like a lifetime ago.

CHAPTER 36 | *Summing it Up*

I ended my nursing career after taking care of an elderly lady for almost four years. By then, I was in a total state of exhaustion and collapse. I'd fallen and broken a foot at one point and limped over to care for my patient until her daughter could get a replacement.

One morning, I couldn't get out of bed. I called Ruthie, our former renter who still lived close by. I asked her to drive me to my doctor at the Motion Picture Hospital in Woodland Hills. I barely got the doctor's office before I collapsed. My blood pressure was pushing me close to having a stroke.

After I retired from nursing, I didn't know what I'd do for money or how I would manage to live and keep my home. I rented my two empty bedrooms for small income and applied for Social Security, which paid me $101 a month. It seemed a ridiculous amount, after all my years of work in films.

Renting part of my house kept me from being alone and I seemed to attract many nice, young fellows. Some stayed with me for years. I guess I became sort of their house mother.

I have kept up with few of my fellow film players over the years. As I said, I rarely made friends

My agent, Don Marlowe, and I at my own star on Hollywood Boulevard in the late 1960s.

with anyone in the entertainment industry. The exceptions were Roy and Dale Evans Rogers and Jack Oakie. Jack and I appeared together in *If I Had a Million* and *The Toast of New York*. In his later years, his wife, Vickie,[1] used to invite some of his friends over for casual get-togethers. Jack's hearing was getting bad, so we did most of the listening while letting him talk over the old times. He enjoyed looking over movie stills, so I'd take my bag of photos for him to browse through.

Vickie once asked me to do an oil portrait of Jack as a surprise gift for his birthday. We chose a photo of him in a sailor cap with a typical Oakie grin to do my portrait from. It turned out quite well, we thought.

[1] Actress Victoria Horne Oakie

I've been asked over the years what had been most satisfying in my life: the film career or my fling with nursing. I wouldn't know how to weigh the satisfaction of one type of work against the other.

The film career gave me recognition throughout the world that I never would have had otherwise. Some years back, I even had my star placed along the Walk of Fame on Hollywood Boulevard with so many greats. I was honored to be

Another self portrait from the 1930s.

remembered for my 200 film portrayals that gave movie fans pleasure and laughter over the world. And, there was not a dirty scene among them. Not many of today's stars can say!

The nursing career gave me a blessing of another type. It was an opportunity for me to show God's love and care for a hurting humanity. What a joy it was to show compassion for my fellow man and to help with physical needs, wounded

A self-portrait of me as I appeared in Artists and Models Abroad. Painting is one of my favorite pastimes.

hearts, and troubled hearts minds.

My Christian faith has meant more to me than anything else this life has had to offer, for it has carried me through all the joys and sorrows and experiences of this life.

The years seem to be rolling by faster and faster now. When I was stronger, I did all my own yard work and would be high up on ladders painting every area of the house I could reach. Now, I have to hurry, sit down, and just smell the flowers before I fall. And, I seem to be doing a lot of that, too.

I now hire workers to do the yard. It keeps me in contact with people, and in some cases, helps me lend a helping hand. Not long ago, I contacted an agency to send someone over to do the yard. He showed up dead drunk. He couldn't work, of course. I was a nurse maid and listened to his problems. I fixed him hot food and tea and put him to bed on the porch lounge. He'd lost his jacket and sweater on the bus. I covered him up and he must have slept three or four hours. I found a warm shirt to send him off in and tucked some money for bus fare in his pocket. I did all the yard work the next day by myself!

Norma Anderson (left) is a long-time friend.

I spend a lot of time writing to fans from all over the world who write with loving memories of Joycie's screen capers. I take personal interest in their lives and some have become closer friends to me than many I've known in Hollywood.

In a way, my mailbox has become a great part of my social life, as I do not "run about." I prefer my quiet home pleasures. I'm a very private person and have to put limits on what I'm willing to do.

For example, I'm concerned, plus annoyed and harassed, when people land on my doorstep and hang around for a half hour or so knocking on my door and calling my name with persistence. I stay quiet, of course. They stand in the driveway, staring up at my window. Once, I crawled out of bed and went to the window and yelled down that I was ill and to please leave. Some even leave notes on the door with phone numbers. It seems ridiculous at this stage in the game.

A woman in New Jersey started writing and sending expensive boxes of cosmetics and vitamins. I wrote and told her to stop with the gifts. She insisted she fly here, move in and take care of me, and repair things with the house. Mercy! I hear that some former film actresses have had to go to court to keep from being annoyed.

My kitty pal, Taj, named for the beautiful Taj Mahal, is one of my pleasures. I take him walking in the jeweled harness I made him. He is a showpiece and car stopper who will happily munch grass and allow passersby to pat and stroke him.

I think Taj, as I've watched him grow up and old over the years, has given me more laughs than anyone I've known. I got him when he was seven weeks old. He's now my 16-year-old teenager. I think he is staying around just to keep me company while I'm still here.

On the rare occasion that I go out for a social event, usually to functions over the holidays, I always dress down with my flamboyant light hair, curls, and ribbons. I don't want to look *too much* at my age.

I've never been to a hair salon in my life. I always created my own hairstyles, from the Tulsa years in my teens, throughout my career, and now. It is important to me to do what suits my type and what is becoming and original. I've never understood why women never seem to be able to take care of their own hair or know what to do with it. Then, I'm amazed at husbands shelling out lots of money to keep their women in shape.

If I get myself fixed up too colorfully, I feel I look like Bette

Taj and I have traveled a long way together.

Davis playing Baby Jane Hudson. I, at least, wear very little makeup. I dislike the plastered or clown look with wild, blue eyelids and false eyelashes, à la Lucille Ball. All that makes the person look too harsh and much older. I much prefer the Helen Hayes simplicity in appearance.

Writing this account of my life, detailing the adventures of the real Joyce Compton, has been exhausting. I had no idea it would be this hard reliving events that I'd put behind me. Strange, when I've never dwelt on the past or been interested in reliving any of those often hectic times and experiences. Here, I got myself all involved, digging it all up again and writing about it. However, once I put pen to paper, I couldn't let it go until I'd shared it all.

Just five months ago, I used to have time to go out and smell the flowers or walk Taj. Or, I'd do some small art project, see a television program, or take a nap. Now, in writing the story of my life, I take a break, open a can of soup, and feed my Taj. Then, I climb the stairs, pick up the pen again, and start picking my brain and browsing in my computer memory.

Interviewers often asked what has been most important to me. First, were my parents; second, is the home we built together. My movie career was hard, and I thank my mom for her idea and vision of getting me into it, for her endless encouragement and prayer, and her script-cueing as we drove to the studios. I also couldn't have made it without my dear, loyal, helpful dad, for his faithfulness to us and for driving me all hours of the night in cold and rain. We were a team. I give them all the credit.

An old friend said the other day that she loves me because I am so unique. I thought about it for a minute, then replied, "Yes, I'm so unique, I'm practically a peculiarity."

Over many decades, many of you got to know me as a movie personality on the big screen. Some of you have gotten to know the celluloid me in recent years thanks to cable, video, and other technologies. Well, now, after reading the pages in this book, you know the real Joyce Compton behind my dumb blonde movie image. I just hope I'm not a disappointment.

PART IV | *Filmography*

Note: The films are listed by year of release. The studio is in parenthesis, following the film title, with the cast listed following the director's credit.

1925

The Golden Bed (Famous Players-Lasky) *D: Cecil B. De Mille.* Lillian Rich, Vera Reynolds, Henry Walthall, Rod La Rocque, Theodore Kosloff, Warner Baxter, Robert Cain, Julia Faye, Robert Edeson, Jacqueline Wells, Mary Jane Irving, Charles Clary, Joyce Compton, Charles Farrell.

Sally (First National) *D: Alfred E. Green.* Colleen Moore, Lloyd Hughes, Leon Errol, Dan Mason, John T. Murray, Eve Novak, Ray Hallor, Carlo Schipa, Myrtle Stedman, Capt. E. H. Calvert, Louise Beaudet, Joyce Compton

Broadway Lady (R-C Pictures) *D: Wesley Ruggles.* Evelyn Brent, Marjorie Bonner, Theodore von Eltz, Joyce Compton, Clarissa Selwynne, Ernest Hilliard, Johnny Gough.

What Fools Men (First National) *D: George Archainbaud.* Lewis Stone, Shirley Mason, Ethel Gray Terry, Barbara Bedford, John Patrick, Hugh Allan, David Torrence, Lewis Dayton, Joyce Compton.

1926

Syncopating Sue (First National) *D: Richard Wallace.* Corinne Griffith, Tom Moore, Rockcliffe Fellowes, Lee Moran, Joyce Compton, Sunshine Hart, Marjorie Rambeau.

1927

Ankles Preferred (Fox) *D: J.G. Blystone.* Madge Bellamy, Lawrence Gray, Barry Norton, Allan Forrest, Marjorie Beebe, Joyce Compton, J. Farrell MacDonald, William Strauss, Lillian Elliott, Mary Foy.

The Border Cavalier (Universal) *D: William Wyler.* Fred Humes, Evelyn Pierce, C.E. "Captain" Anderson, Boris Bullock, Joyce Compton, Dick LaReno, Dick L'Estrange, Gilbert "Pee Wee" Holmes, Benny Corbett.

1928

Soft Living (Fox) *D: James Tinling.* Madge Bellamy, Johnny Mack Brown, Mary Duncan, Joyce Compton, Thomas Jefferson, Henry Kolker, Olive Tell.

1929

The Wild Party (Paramount) *D: Dorothy Arzner.* Clara Bow, Fredric March, Marceline Day, Jack Oakie, Shirley O'Hara, Joyce Compton, Adrienne Dore, Virginia Thomas, Jean Lorraine, Kay Bryant, Alice Adair, Renee Whitney, Amo Ingram, Marguerite Carmer, Phillips R. Holmes, Ben Hendricks, Jr., Jack Luden, Jack Raymond.

Dangerous Curves (Paramount) *D: Lothar Mendes.* Clara Bow, Richard Arlen, Kay Francis, David Newell, Anders Randolf, May Boley, T. Roy Barnes, Joyce Compton, Charles D. Brown, Stuart Erwin, Jack Luden, Oscar Smith, Ethan Laidlaw, Russ Powell.

Salute (Fox) *D: John Ford.* George O'Brien, Helen Chandler, Frank Albertson, William Janney, Joyce Compton, David Butler, Stepin Fetchit, Clifford Dempsey, Lumsden Hare, Rex Bell, John Breeden, John Wayne, Ward Bond.

1930

The Sky Hawk (Fox) *D: John G. Blystone.* Helen Chandler, John Garrick, Gilbert Emery, Lennox Pawle, Lumsden Hare, Billy Bevan, Joyce Compton, Daphne Pollard, Percy Challenger.

High Society Blues (Fox) *D: David Butler.* Janet Gaynor, Charles Farrell, William Collier Sr., Hedda Hopper, Joyce Compton, Lucien Littlefield, Louise Fazenda, Brandon Hurst, Gregory Gaye.

The Three Sisters (Fox) *D: Paul Sloane.* Louise Dresser, Tom Patricola, Kenneth MacKenna, June Collyer, Joyce Compton, Addie McPhail, Clifford Saum, Sidney DeGray, Paul Porcasi, John St. Polis, Herman Bing.

Wild Company (Fox) *D: Leo McCarey.* H. B. Warner, Frank Albertson, Sharon Lynn, Joyce Compton, Claire McDowell, Mildred Van Dorn, Richard Keene, Bela Lugosi, Frances McCoy, Kenneth Thomson, Bobby Callahan, George Fawcett.

Lightnin' (Fox) *D: Henry King.* Will Rogers, Louise Dresser, Joel McCrea, Helen Cohan, Joyce Compton, Jason Robards, Luke Cosgrove, J.M. Kerrigan, Ruth Warren, Sharon Lynn, Rex Bell, Frank Campeau, Goodee Montgomery, Philip Tead, Walter Percival, Charlotte Walker, Blanche LeClair, Bruce Warren, Antica Nast, Moon Carroll, Bess Flowers, Gwendolyn Faye, Eva Dennison, Betty Alden, Lucille Young, Betty Sinclair, Roxanne Curtis, Thomas Jefferson.

Joan Marsh, Joyce, and Loretta Young in Three Girls Lost.

1931

Not Exactly Gentlemen (Fox) *D: Ben Stoloff.* Victor McLaglen, Fay Wray, Robert Warwick, Lew Cody, Eddie Gribbon, David Worth, Joyce Compton, Louise Huntington, Franklyn Franum. Carol Wines, James Farley.

Three Girls Lost (Fox) *D: Sidney Lanfield.* Loretta Young, John Wayne, Lew Cody, Joan Marsh, Joyce Compton, Kathrin Clare Ward, Paul Fix, Bert Roach.

The Spider (Fox) *D: William C. Menzies and Kenneth MacKenna.* Edmund Lowe, Lois Moran, El Brendel, John Arledge, George E. Stone, Earle Foxe, Manya Roberti, Howard Phillips, Purnell Pratt, William Pawley, Joyce Compton, Warren Hymer, Ward Bond.

Up Pops the Devil (Paramount) *D: A. Edward Sutherland.* Richard "Skeets" Gallagher, Stuart Erwin, Carole Lombard, Lilyan Tashman, Joyce Compton, Norman Foster, Edward J. Nugent, Theodore von Eltz, Eulalie Jensen, Harry Beresford, Effie Ellsler, Sleep 'n' Eat (Willie Best), Guy Oliver, Pat Moriarity, Matty Roubert.

Joyce and Helen Chandler in Lena Rogers. COURTESY OF MATT HINRICHS.

Women of All Nations (Fox) *D: Raoul Walsh.* Victor McLaglen, Edmund Lowe, Greta Nissen, Fifi D'Orsay, Joyce Compton, Marjorie White, T. Roy Barnes, Bela Lugosi, Humphrey Bogart, Jesse DeVorska, Charles Judels, Marion Lessing, Ruth Warren.

Annabelle's Affairs (Fox) *D: Alfred Werker.* Victor McLaglen, Jeanette MacDonald, Roland Young, Sally Blane, Joyce Compton, Sam Hardy, William Collier Sr., Ruth Warren, George Andre Beranger, Walter Walker, Hank Mann, Jed Prouty, Louise Beavers, Wilbur Mack.

Good Sport (Fox) *D: Kenneth MacKenna.* Linda Watkins, John Boles, Greta Nissen, Hedda Hopper, Joyce Compton, Minna Gombell, Alan Dinehart, Claire Maynard, Ethel Kenyon, Louise Beavers, Sally Blane, Betty Francisco, Eleanor Hunt, Christine Maple, Geneva Mitchell, Nadine Dore.

1932

Under 18 (Warner Bros.) *D: Archie Mayo.* Marian Marsh, Anita Page, Regis Toomey, Warren William, Joyce Compton, Emma Dunn, J. Farrell MacDonald, Judith Vosselli, Norman Foster, Dorothy Appleby, Maude Eburne, Claire Dodd, Paul Porcasi, Mary Doran, Murray Kinnell, Walter McGrail, Dorothy Granger.

Wheeler Oakman, Dorothy Revier, Harry C. Bradley, and Joyce in Beauty Parlor. COURTESY OF
MATT HINRICHS.

Lena Rivers (Tiffany) *D: Phil Rosen.* Charlotte Henry, Beryl Mercer, James
Kirkwood, Morgan Galloway, Betty Blythe, John St. Polis, Joyce Compton,
Clarence Muse, John Larkin, Russell Simpson, The Kentucky Jubilee Singers.

Westward Passage (RKO) *D: Robert Milton.* Ann Harding, Laurence Olivier,
ZaSu Pitts, Bonita Granville, Irving Pichel, Juliette Compton, Irene Purcell,
Emmett King, Florence Roberts, Ethel Griffies, Don Alvarado, Florence Lake,
Edgar Kennedy, Herman Bing, Julie Haydon, Joyce Compton, Nance O'Neill.

Unholy Love (Allied) *D: Albert Ray.* H. B. Warner, Lila Lee, Beryl Mercer, Lyle
Talbot, Joyce Compton, Ivan Lebedeff, Jason Robards, Kathlyn Williams.

Beauty Parlor (Chesterfield) *D: Richard Thorpe.* Barbara Kent, John Harron,
Dorothy Revier, Mischa Auer, Joyce Compton, John Harron, Betty Mack,
Wheeler Oakman, Albert Gran, Harry C. Bradley.

Lady and Gent (Paramount) *D: Stephen Roberts.* George Bancroft, Wynne Gibson,
James Gleason, John Wayne, Joyce Compton, Charles Starrett, Morgan Wallace,
Billy Butts.

Gary Cooper and Joyce in If I Had a Million.

Fighting for Justice (Columbia) *D: Otto Brower.* Tim McCoy, Robert Frazer, William V. Mong, Hooper Atchley, Joyce Compton, William Norton Bailey, Walter Brennan, Lafe McKee, Harry Todd, Harry Cording, Murdoch McQuarrie, Charles King.

A Parisian Romance (Allied) *D: Chester M. Franklin.* Lew Cody, Marion Shilling, Gilbert Roland, Yola D'Avril, Joyce Compton, Luis Alberni, Nadine Dore, James Eagle, Bryant Washburn, Helen Jerome Eddy, Oscar Apfel, Nicholas Soussanin, George Lewis, Paul Porcasi.

Hat Check Girl (Fox) *D: Sidney Lanfield.* Sally Eilers, Ben Lyon, Ginger Rogers, Monroe Owsley, Arthur Pierson, Noel Madison, Purnell Pratt, Dewey Robinson, Harold Goodwin, Eulalie Jensen, Henry Armetta, Edwin Brady, Hooper Atchley, Richard Carle, Bud Flanagan, Gordan "Bill" Elliott, Bert Roach, Arthur Housman, Eddie Anderson, Lee Moran, Harry Schultz, Joyce Compton, Astrid Allwyn, Sherry Hall, Harvey Clark.

False Faces (World Wide) *D: Lowell Sherman.* Lowell Sherman, Lila Lee, Peggy Shannon, Berton Churchill, Joyce Compton, Geneva Mitchell, David Landau, Harold Waldridge, Nance O'Neil, Purnell Pratt, Olive Tell, Forrest Stanley, Oscar Apfel, Miriam Seegar.

Madison Sq. Garden (Paramount) *D: Harry Joe Brown.* Jack Oakie, Thomas Meighan, Marion Nixon, Lew Cody, William Collier, Sr., ZaSu Pitts, William Boyd, Warren Hymer, Robert Elliott, Joyce Compton, Bert Gordon, Noel Francis.

Afraid to Talk (Universal) *D: Edward L. Cahn.* Sidney Fox, Eric Linden, Tully Marshall, Louis Calhern, Robert Warwick, Berton Churchill, Edward Arnold, George Meeker, Mayo Methot, Ian MacLaren, Matt McHugh, Frank Sheridan, Thomas Jackson, Gusav von Seyffertitz, Reginald Barlow, Edward Martindel, Joyce Compton, John Ince, George Chandler, Arthur Housman.

If I Had a Million (Paramount) *D: Ernst Lubitsch, Norman Taurog, Stephen Roberts, Norman McLeod, James Cruze, William A. Seiter, H. Bruce Humberstone.* Gary Cooper, Charles Laughton, George Raft, W. C. Fields, Joyce Compton, Wynne Gibson, Jack Oakie, Frances Dee, Charles Ruggles, Alison Skipworth, Mary Boland, Roscoe Karns, May Robson, Gene Raymond, Lucien Littlefield, Richard Bennett, Grant Mitchell, Cecil Cunningham, Irving Bacon, Blanche Frederici, Dewey Robinson, Gail Patrick, Fred Kelsey, Willard Robertson, Kent Taylor, Jack Pennick, Berton Churchill, James Burtis.

1933

Only Yesterday (Universal) *D: John M. Stahl.* Margaret Sullavan, John Boles, Billie Burke, Reginald Denny, Jimmy Butler, Edna May Oliver, Benita Hume, George Meeker, June Clyde, Marie Prevost, Oscar Apfel, Jane Darwell, Tom Conlon, Berton Churchill, Onslow Stevens, Franklin Pangborn, Walter Catlett, Noel Francis, Barry Norton, Arthur Hoyt, Natalie Moorhead, Joyce Compton, Betty Blythe, Grady Sutton, Ruth Clifford, Julia Faye, Crauford Kent, Vivian Oakland, Dorothy Christy, Bramwell Fletcher, Dorothy Granger, Geneva Mitchell, Bert Roach, Louise Beavers.

Sing, Sinner, Sing (Majestic) *D: Howard Christy.* Paul Lukas, Leila Hyams, Donald Dillaway, Ruth Donnelly, Joyce Compton, George E. Stone, Jill Dennett, Arthur Hoyt, Walter McGrail, Gladys Blake, Arthur Housman, Edgar Norton, John St. Polis, Stella Adams, Pat O'Malley, Walter Brennan, Walter Humphrey.

Caliente Love (Sennett, short) Walter Catlett, Eddie Nugent, Mona Maris, Paul Porcasi, Joyce Compton.

The Wrestlers (Sennett, short) Eddie Gribbon, Joyce Compton.

Dream Stuff (Sennett, short) Walter Catlett, Emerson Treacy, Franklin Pangborn, Al Cooke, Joyce Compton.

Knockout Kisses (Sennett, short) Richard Hemingway, Bud Jamison, Matt McHugh, Joyce Compton.

The Plumber and the Lady (Sennett, short) Frank Albertson, Marjorie Beebe, Herman Bing, Gertrude Astor, Joyce Compton.

Roadhouse Queen (Sennett, short) Walter Catlett, Joyce Compton, Ben Alexander, Nora Lane, Arthur Housman.

Daddy Knows Best (Sennett, short) Walter Catlett, Joyce Compton, Ben Alexander, Dorothy Granger.

The Big Fibber (Sennett, short) Walter Catlett, Joyce Compton, Elise Cavanna, Billy Gilbert, Grady Sutton.

1934

Everything's Ducky (RKO, short) Bobby Clark, Joyce Compton, Paul McCullough, Eddie Gribbon, Maude Truax.

The Trumpet Blows (Paramount) *D: Stephen Roberts*. George Raft, Adolph Menjou, Frances Drake, Sidney Toler, Edward Ellis, Nydia Westman, Douglas Wood, Lillian Elliott, Katherine De Mille, Francis McDonald, Morgan Wallace, Gertrude Norman, Joyce Compton.

Affairs of a Gentleman (Universal) *D: Edwin L. Marin*. Paul Lukas, Leila Hyams, Patricia Ellis, Philip Reed, Onslow Stevens, Dorothy Burgess, Lilian Bond, Joyce Compton, Murray Kinnell, Dorothy Libaire, Richard Carle, Wilfred Hari, Sara Haden, Charles Wilson, Gregory Gaye.

Million Dollar Ransom (Universal) *D: Murray Roth*. Phillips Holmes, Edward Arnold, Andy Devine, Mary Carlisle, Wini Shaw, Robert Gleckler, Marjorie Gateson, Edgar Norton, Bradley Page, Hughey White, Charles Coleman, Henry Kolker, Jane Darwell, Jay C. Flippen, Spencer Charters, Joyce Compton.

King Kelly of the U.S.A. (Monogram) *D: Leonard Fields*. Guy Robertson, Edgar Kennedy, Irene Ware, Joyce Compton, Franklin Pangborn, Ferdinand Gottschalk, William Von Brincken, Lorin Raker, Otis Harlan, Bodil Rosing.

The White Parade (Fox) *D: Irving Cummings.* Loretta Young, John Boles, Dorothy Wilson, Muriel Kirkland, Joyce Compton, Jane Darwell, Sarah Haden, Astrid Allwyn, Jean Barnes, Frank Conroy, Noel Francis, Polly Ann Young, June Gittelson.

Imitation of Life (Universal) *D: John M. Stahl.* Claudette Colbert, Warren William, Louise Beavers, Fredi Washington, Ned Sparks, Baby Jane "Juanita" Quigley, Marilyn Knowlden, Rochelle Hudson, Fredi Washington, Alan Hale, Clarence Wilson, Henry Armetta, Henry Kolker, Wyndham Standing, Paul Porcasi, Alice Ardell, Noel Francis, William Davidson, Walter Walker, Franklin Pangborn, Edgar Norton, Joyce Compton, Barry Norton, Madame Su-Te-Wan, Claire McDowell, Fred Toones, Hattie McDaniel, Dennis O'Keefe.

1935

Rustlers of Red Dog (Universal, 12-chapter serial) *D: Louis Friedlander (Lew Landers).* Johnny Mack Brown, Joyce Compton, Raymond Hatton, Walter Miller, Harry Woods, Fredric MacKaye, Charles K. French, William Desmond, Chief Thundercloud, Slim Whitaker, Art Mix, Jim Corey, Bill Patton, Cliff Lyons, Tex Cooper, Ben Corbett, Hank Bell, Bud Osborne, Edmund Cobb, J.P. McGowan, Monte

Joyce as Mary Lee in Rustlers of Red Dog.
COURTESY OF MATT HINRICHS.

Montague, Lafe McKee, Artie Artego, Jim Thorpe, Chief Thunderbird, Ann Darcy, Fritzi Brunette, Grace Cunard, Virginia Ainsworth, Iron Eyes Cody, Chief Miny Treaties. *Chapters: Hostile Redskins, Flaming Arrows, Thundering Hoofs, Attack at Dawn, Buried Alive, Flames of Vengeance, Into the Depths, Paths of Peril, The Snake Strikes, Riding Wild, The Rustler's Clash, Law and Order.*

Go Into Your Dance (First National) *D: Archie Mayo.* Al Jolson, Ruby Keeler, Glenda Farrell, Barton MacLane, Benny Rubin, Phil Regan, Sharon Lynn, William Davidson, Akim Tamiroff, Helen Morgan, Harry Warren, Gordon Westcott, Patsy Kelly, Joyce Compton, Joseph Cawthorn.

Advertisement for Suicide Squad.
COURTESY OF MATT HINRICHS.

Mr. Dynamite (Universal) *D: Alan Crosland.* Edmund Lowe, Jean Dixon, Victor Varconi, Esther Ralston, Verna Hillie, Minor Watson, Robert Gleckler, Jameson Thomas, Matt McHugh, G. Pat Collins, Greta Meyer, Bradley Page, James Burtis, Joyce Compton.

Let 'Em Have It (United Artists) *D: Sam Wood.* Richard Arlen, Virginia Bruce, Alice Brady, Bruce Cabot, Harvey Stephens, Eric Linden, Joyce Compton, Gordon Jones, J. Farrell MacDonald, Bodil Rosing, Paul Stanton, Robert Emmett O'Connor, Hale Hamilton, Dorothy Appleby, Barbara Pepper, Matthew Betz, Harry Woods, Clyde Dilson, Matty Fain, Paul Fix, Donald Kirke, Eugene Strong, Christian Rub, Eleanor Wesselhoeft, Wesley Barry, Ian MacLaren, George Pauncefort, Joseph King, Clarence Wilson, Arthur Hoyt.

College Scandal (Paramount) *D: Elliott Nugent.* Arline Judge, Kent Taylor, Wendy Barrie, William Frawley, William Benedict, Mary Nash, Benny Baker, Edward Nugent, William Stack, Johnny Downs, Douglas Blackley, Joyce Compton, Samuel S. Hinds, Douglas Wood, Edith Arnold, Helena Phillips Evans, Mary Ellen Brown, Stanley Andrews, Sam Godfrey, Oscar Smith, Oscar Rudolph.

Magnificent Obsession (Universal) *D: John M. Stahl.* Irene Dunne, Robert Taylor, Charles Butterworth, Betty Furness, Sara Haden, Ralph Morgan, Henry Armetta, Crauford Kent, Edward Earle, Inez Courtney, Beryl Mercer, Cora Cue Collins, Arthur Treacher, Joyce Compton, Walter Miller, Mickey Daniels

E.E. Clive and Joyce in Love Before Breakfast.

School for Girls (Liberty) *D: William High.* Sidney Fox, Paul Kelly, Lois Wilson, Lucille LaVerne, Dorothy Lee, Toby Wing, Dorothy Appleby, Lona Andre, Joyce Compton, Russell Hopton, Anna Q. Nilsson, Barbara Weeks, Kathleen Burke, William Farnum, Charles Ray, Mary Foy, Dawn O'Day, Myrtle Stedman, Helene Chadwick.

Suicide Squad (Puritain) *D: Raymond K. Johnson.* Norman Foster, Robert Homans, Aggie Herring, Joyce Compton, Phil E. Kramer, Peter Warren, Jack Luden.

Manhattan Monkey Business (MGM, short) Charley Chase, James Finlayson, Milton Owen, Joyce Compton, Gertrude Astor.

Life Hesitates at 40 (MGM, short) Charley Chase, James Finlayson, Brooks Benedict, Joyce Compton, Carl "Alfalfa" Switzer.

Public Ghost No. 1 (MGM, short) Charley Chase, Edwin Maxwell, Clarence Wilson, Joyce Compton, Ray Turner.

Lyle Talbot, Mary Astor, Joyce, and Nat Pendleton in Trapped by Television.

Hollywood Hobbies (MGM, short) Sally Payne, William Benedict, James Stewart, Joyce Compton, Clark Gable.

1936

Valley of the Lawless (Supreme) *D: Robert N. Bradbury.* Johnny Mack Brown, Joyce Compton, George Hayes, Frank Hagney, Joyce Compton, Dennis Meadows (Moore), Bobby Nelson, Charles King, Jack Rockwell, Frank Ball, Bob McKenzie, Milburn Morante, Forrest Taylor, Jack Evans, Rube Dalroy, Tex Phelps, Anita Camargo.

Love Before Breakfast (Universal) *D: Walter Lang.* Carole Lombard, Preston Foster, Cesar Romero, Janet Beecher, Betty Lawford, Douglas Blackley, Don Briggs, Bert Roach, Andre Beranger, Richard Carle, Ed Barton, Diana Gibson, Joyce Compton, John King, E. E. Clive, Forrester Harvey, John Rogers.

Three Smart Girls (Universal) *D: Michael Curtiz.* Binnie Barnes, Charles Winninger, Alice Brady, Ray Milland, Mischa Auer, Ernest Cossart, Lucile Watson, John King, Nella Walker, Hobart Cavanaugh, Nan Gray, Barbara Read, Deanna Durbin, Joyce Compton.

The Harvester (Republic) *D: Joseph Santley.* Alice Brady, Russell Hardie, Ann Rutherford, Joyce Compton, Frank Craven, Cora Sue Collins, Emma Dunn, Eddie Nugent, Roy Atwell, Spencer Charters, Russell Simpson, Phyllis Fraser, Fern Emmett, Burr Caruth, Lucille Ward, Harry Brown, Grace Hale.

Trapped by Television (Columbia) *D: Del Lord.* Mary Astor, Lyle Talbot, Nat Pendleton, Joyce Compton, Thurston Hall, Henry Mollison, Wyrley Birch, Robert Strange, Marc Lawrence.

Star for a Night (20th Century-Fox) *D: Lewis Seiler* Claire Trevor, Jane Darwell, Evelyn Venable, Joyce Compton, Arline Judge, J. Edward Bromberg, Frank Reicher, Astrid Allwyn, Dean Jagger, Adrienne Marden, Susan Fleming, Dickie Walters, Chick Chandler, Hattie McDaniel, Alan Dinehart.

Sitting on the Moon (Republic) *D: Ralph Staub.* Roger Pryor, Grace Bradley, Joyce Compton, William Newell, Henry Kolker, Pert Kelton, Henry Wadsworth, Pierre Watkin, William Janney, June Martel, The Theodores, Jimmy Ray, Harvey Clark, George Cooper.

Ellis Island (Chesterfield) *D: Phil Rosen.* Donald Cook, Peggy Shannon, Joyce Compton, Jack LaRue, Bradley Page, Johnny Arthur, Maurice Black, Bryant Washburn, Robert Frazer.

Under Your Spell (20th Century-Fox) *D: Otto Preminger.* Lawrence Tibbett, Wendy Barrie, Gregory Ratoff, Arthur Treacher, Gregory Gaye, Berton Churchill, Jed Prouty, Claudia Coleman, Charles Richman, Madge Bellamy, Nora Cecil, Bobby Samarzich, Joyce Compton, June Gittelson.

Country Gentleman (Republic) *D: Ralph Staub.* Ole Olsen, Chic Johnson, Lila Lee, Joyce Compton, Pierre Watkin, Donald Kirke, Ray Corrigan, Sammy McKim, Wade Boteler, Ivan Miller, Olin Howard, Frank Sheridan, Harry Harvey, Joe Cunningham.

Murder with Pictures (Paramount) *D: Charles Barton.* Lew Ayres, Gail Patrick, Paul Kelly, Joyce Compton, Onslow Stevens, Ernest Cossart, Anthony Nace, Benny Baker, Joseph Sawyer.

1937

China Passage (RKO) *D: Edward Killy.* Constance Worth, Vinton Haworth, Leslie Fenton, Gordon Jones, Alec Craig, Dick Elliott, Frank M. Thomas, George Irving, Billy Gilbert, Joyce Compton, Phillip Ahn, Lotus Long, Lotus Liu, Tetsu Komai, Moy Ming, Huntley Gordan, Anita Colby, William Corson, Alan Curtis.

Top of the Town (Universal) *D: Ralph Murphy.* Doris Nolan, George Murphy, Joyce Compton, Mischa Auer, Ella Logan, Gertrude Niesen, Claude Gillingwater, Richard Carle, Samuel S. Hinds, Ray Mayer, Hugh Herbert, Peggy Ryan, Gregory Ratoff, Henry Armetta.

Pick a Star (MGM) *D: Edward Sedgwick.* Patsy Kelly, Jack Haley, Mischa Auer, Rosina Lawrence, Joyce Compton, Lyda Roberti, Charles Halton, Russell Hicks, Spencer Charters, James Finlayson, Walter Long, James C. Morton, Barbara Weeks, Si Jenks, Wilbur Mack, Bob O'Connor, Sam Adams, Wesley Barry, Johnny Hyams, Leila McIntyre, Stan Laurel, Oliver Hardy.

Kid Galahad (Warner Bros.) *D: Michael Curtiz.* Edward G. Robinson, Bette Davis, Humphrey Bogart, Wayne Morris, Jane Bryan, Harry Carey, William Haade, Soledad Jiminez, Joe Cunningham, Ben Welden, Joseph Crehan, Veda Ann Borg, Frank Faylen, Joyce Compton, George Blake, Charles Sullivan.

Rhythm in the Clouds (Republic) *D: John H. Auer.* Patricia Ellis, Warren Hull, Joyce Compton, William Newell, Richard Carle, David Carlyle, Zeffie Tilbury, Esther Howard, Charles Judels, Richard Beach, Ranny Weeks, Rolfe Sedan, Billy Benedict.

Born Reckless (20th Century-Fox) *D: Malcolm St. Clair.* Rochelle Hudson, Brian Donlevy, Barton MacLane, Robert Kent, Harry Carey, Pauline Moore, Chick Chandler, William Pawley, Francis McDonald, Joyce Compton.

The Toast of New York (RKO) *D: Rowland V. Lee.* Edward Arnold, Cary Grant, Frances Farmer, Jack Oakie, Donald Meek, Thelma Leeds, Clarence Kolb, Robert McClung, Dudley Clements, Marie Marks, Ginger Connolly, Joseph De Stefani, Ted Thompson, Jack Luden, Reed Howes, Wally Dean, Jay Eaton, Fred Lee, Crauford Kent, Otto Hoffman, Winter Hall, Frank Darien, Earl Dwire, George Cleveland, Ben Hall, James Finlayson, Frank Swales, Foy Van Dolsen, Lon Poff, Frank Hammond, Nelson McDowell, Clem Bevans, Maxine Elliott Hicks, Daisy Bufford, Stanley Blystone, Jack Kenny, Chris Frank, Frank Rasmussen,

Robert Dudley, Mary Gordon, Dewey Robinson, Reginald Barlow, Nick Thompson, Jack Egan, Margaret Morris, Oscar Apfel, Tom Brewer, George Irving, Jack Carson, Eddie Hart, Bentley Hewlett, Harvey Clark, Frank Hall Crane, Russell Hicks, Joyce Compton, Virginia Carroll, Tom Coleman, James Mason, Dick Kipling, George Lollier.

Sea Racketeers (Republic) *D: Hamilton McFadden.* Weldon Heyburn, Jeanne Madden, Warren Hymer, Joyce Compton, Dorothy McNulty (Penny Singleton), J. Carrol Naish, Charles Trowbridge, Bennie Burt, Sid Saylor, Ralph Sanford, Don Rowan, Anthony Pawley, Bobby Hale, Sam Flint, Bryant Washburn, Christine McIntyre, Paul Renay, Lew Harvey, Lane Chandler, Henry Rocquemore.

Advertisement for Small Town Boy. COURTESY OF MATT HINRICHS.

She Asked for It (Paramount) *D: Erle C. Kenton.* William Gargan, Orien Heyward, Vivienne Osborne, Richard Carle, Roland Drew, Harry Beresford, Alan Birmingham, Tully Marshall, Joyce Compton, Nora Cecil, Edward Earle.

Small Town Boy (Grand National) *D: Glenn Tryon.* Stuart Erwin, Jed Prouty, Clara Blandick, Joyce Compton, James Blakeley, Clarence Wilson, Paul Hurst, Edward (Eddy) Waller, Eddie Kane, George Chandler, Victor Potel.

The Awful Truth (Columbia) D: Leo McCarey -- Irene Dunne, Cary Grant, Ralph Bellamy, Alexander D'Arcy, Cecil Cunningham, Joyce Compton, Molly Lamont, Esther Dale, Robert Allen, Robert Warwick, Mary Forbes, Claud Allister, Zita Moulton, Scott Colton, Wyn Cahoon, Paul Stanton, Mitchell Harris, Alan Bridge, Edgar Dearing, Leonard Carey, Miki Morita, Frank Wilson, Vernon Dent, George Pearce, Bobby Watson, Bryon Foulger, Kathryn Curry, Edward Peil, Sr., Bess Flowers, John Tyrrell, Edward Mortimer.

Jacqueline Wells, Joyce Compton, Lew Ayres, Ann Morriss, Ruth Hussey, and Maureen O'Sullivan in Spring Madness. COURTESY OF MATT HINRICHS.

Wings Over Honolulu (Universal) *D: H.C. Potter.* Wendy Barrie, Ray Milland, William Gargan, Kent Taylor, Polly Rowles, Samuel S. Hinds, Mary Philips, Clara Blandick, Margaret McWade, Louise Beavers, Joyce Compton, Robert Spencer, Jonathan Hale, Jack Mulhall, Buddy Messinger, Frank Melton, Grace Cunard, Loretta Sayers, Ray Turner, Louise Latimer, Isabel LaMal, Al Kikume, Martin Turner.

We Have Our Moments (Universal) *D: Alfred L. Werker.* Sally Eilers, James Dunn, Mischa Auer, David Niven, Warren Hymer, Marjorie Gateson, Thurston Hall, Virginia Sale, Joyce Compton, Grady Sutton, Franklin Pangborn, Margaret McWade, Olaf Hytten.

1938

Women Are Like That (Warner Bros.) D: Stanley Logan -- Kay Francis, Pat O'Brien, Ralph Forbes, Melville Cooper, Thurston Hall, Grant Mitchell, Gordon Oliver, John Eldredge, Herbert Rawlinson, Hugh O'Connell, Georgia Caine, Joyce Compton, Sarah Edwards, Josephine Whittell, Loia Cheaney, Edward Broadley.

Man-Proof (MGM) *D: Richard Thorpe.* Myrna Loy, Franchot Tone, Rosalind Russell, Walter Pidgeon, Rita Johnson, Nana Bryant, Ruth Hussey, John Miljan, Joyce Compton, William Stack, Leonard Penn, Oscar O'Shea, Marie Blake, Dan Toby, Aileen Pringle, Grace Hayle, Laura Treadwell, Frances Reid, Betty Blythe, Francis X. Bushman, Jr.

You and Me (Paramount) *D: Fritz Lang.* Sylvia Sidney, George Raft, Barton MacLane, Harry Carey, Robert Cummings, Roscoe Karns, George E. Stone, Warren Hymer, Joyce Compton, Guinn Williams, Carol Page, Bernadine Hayes, Egan Brecher, Paul Newlan, Harlan Briggs, Blanca Vischer, Sheila Darcy, Margaret Randall, Jack Mulhall, Sam Ash, Julia Faye, Arthur Hoyt, Cecil Cunningham, Roger Gray, Adrian Morris, Joe Gray, Jack Pennick, Kit Guard, Fern Emmett, Max Barwyn, James McNamara, Matt McHugh, Richard Denning, Joyce Mathews, William B. Davidson.

Spring Madness (MGM) *D: S. Sylvan Simon.* Maureen O'Sullivan, Lew Ayres, Ruth Hussey, Joyce Compton, Burgess Meredith, Ann Morriss, Frank Albertson, Jacqueline Wells (Julie Bishop), Marjorie Gateson, Sterling Holloway

Artists and Models Abroad (Paramount) *D: Mitchell Leisen.* Jack Benny, Joan Bennett, Mary Boland, Charley Grapewin, Yacht Club Boys, Fritz Feld, Phyllis Kennedy, Monty Woolley, G.P. Huntley, Joyce Compton, Adrienne D'Ambricourt, Andre Cheron, Jules Raucourt, Georges Renavant, Chester Clute, Alex Melesh, Sheila Darcy, Dolores Casey, Yvonne Duval, Marie DeForrest, Gwen Kenyon, Joyce Matthews, Mary Parker .

Trade Winds (United Artists) *D: Tay Garnett.* Fredric March, Joan Bennett, Ralph Bellamy, Ann Sothern, Sidney Blackmer, Thomas Mitchell, Robert Elliott, Richard Tucker, Joyce Compton, Patricia Farr, Wilma Francis, Phyllis Barry, Dorothy Tree, Kay Linaker, Dorothy Comingore (Linda Winters), Walter Byron, Wilson Benge, Hooper Atchley, Lee Phelps, Franklin Parker, John Webb Dillon, Dick Ruch, Jack Baxley, Beryl Wallace, Suzanne Kaaren.

Love on a Budget (20th Century-Fox) *D: Herbert I. Leeds.* Jed Prouty, Shirley Deane, Spring Byington, Russell Gleason, Kenneth Howell, George Ernest, June Carlson, Florence Roberts, Billy Mahan, Alan Dinehart, Dixie Dunbar, Marvin Stephens, Paul Harvey, Joyce Compton.

Al Jolson, Joyce, and Alice Faye in Rose of Washington Square.

Going Places (Warner Bros.) *D: Ray Enright.* Dick Powell, Anita Louise, Allen Jenkins, Ronald Reagan, Joyce Compton, Walter Catlett, Harold Huber, Larry Williams, Thurston Hall, Minna Gombell, Robert Warwick, John Ridgely, Joe Cunningham, Eddie "Rochester" Anderson, George Reed, Louis Armstrong, Maxine Sullivan.

How to Watch Football (MGM, short) Robert Benchley, John Butler, Eddie Acuff, Diane Cook, Joyce Compton.

1939

The Last Warning (Universal) *D: Al Rogell.* Preston Foster, Kay Linaker, Frank Jenks, E. E. Clive, Joyce Compton, Frances Robinson, Ray Parker, Robert Paige, Albert Dekker, Roland Drew, Clem Wilenchick, Orville Caldwell, Richard Lane.

Rose of Washington Square (20th Century-Fox) *D: Gregory Ratoff.* Alice Faye, Tyrone Power, Al Jolson, William Frawley, Joyce Compton, Hobart Cavanaugh, Moroni Olsen, E.E. Clive, Louis Prima, Charles Wilson, Hal K. Dawson, Paul E. Burns, Ben Welden, Horace MacMahon, Paul Stanton, Maurice Cass, Bert Roach, Harry Hayden, Chick Chandler, Murray Alper, Ralph Dunn, Edgar Dearing, Robert Shaw, James Flavin, Adrian Morris, Winifred Harris.

Hotel for Women (20th Century-Fox) *D: Gregory Ratoff.* Ann Sothern, Linda Darnell, James Ellison, Lynn Bari, June Gale, Joyce Compton, Elsa Maxwell, John Halliday, Katherine (Kay) Aldridge, Alan Dinehart, Sidney Blackmer, Mary Healy, Amanda Duff, Chick Chandler, Gregory Gaye, Charles Wilson, Herbert Ashley, Ivan Lebedeff, Helen Ericson, Dorothy Dearing, Barnett Parker, Lillian Porter, Ruth Terry, Kay Griffith, Irma Wilson, Kay Linaker, Claire DuBrey, Charles Trowbridge.

Reno (RKO) *D: John Farrow.* Richard Dix, Gail Patrick, Anita Louise, Paul Cavanaugh, Laura Hope Crews, Louis Jean Heydt, Hobart Cavanaugh, Charles Halton, Astrid Allwyn, Joyce Compton, Frank Faylen, William Haade, Carole Landis, Billie Seward.

Balalaika (MGM) *D: Reinhold Schunzel.* Nelson Eddy, Ilona Massey, Charles Ruggles, Frank Morgan, Joyce Compton, Walter Woolf King, Lionel Atwill, C. Aubrey Smith, Phil Terry, Frederic Worlock, Abner Biberman, Arthur W. Cernitz, Roland Varno, George Tobias, Paul Sutton, Willy Costello, Paul Irving, Alma Kruger, Zeffie Tilbury, Dalies Frantz.

The Flying Irishman (RKO) *D: Leigh Jason.* Douglas Corrigan, Paul Kelly, Gene Reynolds, Lee Phelps, Robert Armstrong, Donald MacBride, Eddie Quillan, J.M. Kerrigan, Dorothy Peterson, Scotty Beckett, Joyce Compton, Dorothy Appleby, Minor Watson, Cora Witherspoon, Spencer Charters, Peggy Ryan.

Escape to Paradise (Principal) *D: Erle C. Kenton.* Bobby Breen, Kent Taylor, Marla Shelton, Joyce Compton, Pedro de Cordoba.

1940

Honeymoon Deferred (Universal) *D: Lew Landers.* Edmund Lowe, Margaret Lindsay, Elisabeth Risdon, Chick Chandler, Joyce Compton, Anne Gwynne, Jerry Marlow, Cliff Clark, Julie Stevens.

Turnabout (United Artists) *D: Hal Roach.* Adolphe Menjou, Carole Landis, John Hubbard, William Gargan, Verree Teasdale, Mary Astor, Donald Meek, Joyce Compton, Inez Courtney, Franklin Pangborn, Marjorie Main, Berton Churchill, Margaret Roach, Ray Turner, Norman Budd, Polly Ann Young, Eleanor Riley, Murray Alper.

Carole Landis, Mary Astor, Royer (fashion designer), and Joyce in Turnabout.

They Drive By Night (Warner Bros.) *D: Raoul Walsh.* George Raft, Humphrey Bogart, Ann Sheridan, Ida Lupino, Gale Page, Alan Hale, Roscoe Karns, John Litel, Henry O'Neill, George Tobias, Charles Halton, Joyce Compton, John Ridgely, Paul Hurst, Charles Wilson, Norman Willis, George Lloyd, Lillian Yarbo, Eddy Chandler, Pedro Regas, Frank Faylen, Ralph Sanford, Sol Gorss, Eddie Fetherston, Vera Lewis.

I Take This Oath (PRC) *D: Sherman Scott (Sam Newfield).* Gordon Jones, Joyce Compton, Craig Reynolds, J. Farrell MacDonald, Robert Homans, Mary Gordon, Sam Flint, Brooks Benedict, Veda Ann Borg, Edward Peil Sr.

City for Conquest (Warner Bros.) *D: Anatole Litvak.* James Cagney, Ann Sheridan, Donald Crisp, Anthony Quinn, Frank McHugh, Fred Craven, Arthur Kennedy, Joyce Compton, George Tobias, Elia Kazan, Jerome Cowan, Lee Patrick, Blanche Yurka, George Lloyd, Thurston Hall, Ben Welden, John Arledge, Edward Keane, Selmer Jackson, Joseph Crehan, Bob Steele, Pat Flaherty, Sidney Miller, Lee Phelps, Howard Hickman, Ed Gargan, Murray Alper, William Newell, Margaret Hayes, Lucia Carroll, Ed Pawley.

Lobby Card for Sky Murder. COURTESY OF MATT HINRICHS.

The Villain Still Pursued Her (RKO) *D: Edward F. Cline.* Hugh Herbert, Anita Louise, Alan Mowbray, Buster Keaton, Joyce Compton, Richard Cromwell, Billy Gilbert, Margaret Hamilton, Diane Fisher, William Farnum, Franklin Pangborn.

Who Killed Aunt Maggie? (Republic) *D: Arthur Lubin.* John Hubbard, Wendy Barrie, Edgar Kennedy, Elizabeth Patterson, Joyce Compton, Onslow Stevens, Walter Abel, Mona Barrie, Willie Best, Daisy Lee Mothershed, Milton Parsons, Tom Dugan, William Haade, Joel Friedkin.

Let's Make Music (RKO) *D: Leslie Goodwins.* Bob Crosby, Jean Rogers, Elisabeth Risdon, Joseph Buloff, Joyce Compton, Bennie Bartlett, Louis Jean Heydt, Bill Goodwin, Frank Orth, Grant Withers, Walter Tetley, Benny Rubin, Jacqueline Nash, Donna Jean Dolfer

Sky Murder (MGM) *D: George B. Seitz.* Walter Pidgeon, Donald Meek, Karen Verne, Edward Ashley, Joyce Compton, Tom Conway, Dorothy Tree, George Lessey, Frank Reicher, Chill Wills, George Watts, Byron Foulger, William Tannen, Milton Parsons, Tom Neal, Lucien Prival.

1940

I Take This Woman (MGM) *D: W.S. Van Dyke.* Spencer Tracy, Hedy Lamarr, Verree Teasdale, Kent Taylor, Laraine Day, Mona Barrie, Jack Carson, Paul Cavanagh, Marjorie Main, Frances Drake, Louis Calhern, George E. Stone, Don Castle, Leon Balsaco, Willie Best, Tom Collins, John Shelton, Gayne Whitman, Charles D. Brown, Joyce Compton, Reed Hadley, Charles Trowbridge, Lee Phelps, Nell Craig, David Clyde, Syd Saylor, Natalie Moorhead, Rafael Storm, Florence Stanley, Esther Michelson, Rosina Galli, Matt McHugh, Peggy Leon.

1941

Ziegfeld Girl (MGM) *D: Robert Z. Leonard, Busby Berkeley.* James Stewart, Judy Garland, Hedy Lamarr, Lana Turner, Tony Martin, Jackie Cooper, Ian Hunter, Charles Winninger, Edward Everett Horton, Philip Dorn, Paul Kelly, Eve Arden, Dan Dailey Jr., Al Shean, Fay Holden, Felix Bressart, Rose Hobart, Bernard Nedell, Edward McNamara, Mae Busch, Jean Wallace, Myrna Dell, Joyce Compton, Bess Flowers.

Manpower (Warner Bros.) *D: Raoul Walsh.* Edward G. Robinson, Marlene Dietrich, George Raft, Alan Hale, Walter Catlett, Frank McHugh, Egon Brecher, Ward Bond, Eve Arden, Joyce Compton, Lucia Carroll, Barbara Pepper, Dorothy Appleby, Joseph Crehan, Cliff Clark, Barton MacLane, Robert Strange, Dick Wessell, Murray Alper, Eddy Chandler, Lee Phelps, Dorothy Vaughn, Roland Drew, William Hooper, Faye Emerson, Isabel Withers, James Flavin, Nella Walker, Ben Welden, Eddie Fetherston, Jeffrey Sayre, Al Herman, Ralph Dunn, Harry Strang, Chester Clute, Harry Holman, Beal Wong, Joyce Bryant.

Scattergood Meets Broadway (RKO) *D: Christy Cabanne.* Guy Kibbee, Mildred Coles, William Henry, Emma Dunn, Joyce Compton, Frank Jenks, Bradley Page, Chester Clute, Morgan Wallace, Charlotte Walker, Carl Stockdale, Paul White, Donald Brodie, Herbert Rawlinson, Sharon Mackie.

Moon Over Her Shoulder (20th Century-Fox) *D: Alfred Werker.* Lynn Bari, John Sutton, Alan Mowbray, Dan Dailey Jr., Leonard Carey, Irving Bacon, Joyce Compton, Lillian Yarbo, Eula Gay, Shirley Hill, Sylvia Arslan.

Blues in the Night (Warner Bros.) *D: Anatole Litvak.* Priscilla Lane, Richard Whorf, Betty Field, Lloyd Nolan, Jack Carson, Elia Kazan, Wallace Ford, Billy Halop, Peter Whitney, Howard de Silva, Herbert Heywood, George Lloyd, Charles Wilson, William Gillespie, Matt McHugh, Joyce Compton, Faye Emerson, Jimmy Lunceford and his Band, Will Osborne and his Band.

Bedtime Story (Columbia) *D: Alexander Hall.* Fredric March, Loretta Young, Robert Benchley, Eve Arden, Joyce Compton, Helen Westley, Tim Ryan, Olaf Hytten, Dorothy Adams, Clarence Kolb, Andrew Tombes, Grady Sutton, Emmett Vogan, Byron Foulger, Spencer Charters, Pierre Watkin, Chester Clute.

1942

Too Many Women (PRC) *D: Bernard B. Ray.* Neil Hamilton, June Lang, Marlo Dwyer, Barbara Read, Joyce Compton, Matt McHugh, Marlo Dwyer, Fred Sherman, Kate McKenna, Maurice Cass, Bertram Marburgh, George Davis, Dora Clement, Harry Holman, Tom Herbert, Pat Gleason, Leonard St. Leo, Frank Hagney, Patsy Moran, Marjorie Haynes, Adele Smith, Adele Kerr, Harry Johnson, Charles Hutchison.

Thunder Birds (20th Century-Fox) *D: William A. Wellman.* Gene Tierney, Preston Foster, John Sutton, Jack Holt, Dame May Whitty, George Barbier, Richard Haydn, Reginald Denny, Ted North, Janis Carter, Joyce Compton, Bess Flowers, Peter Lawford, Selmer Jackson, Charles Tannen, Harry Strang, Walter Tetley, Montague Shaw, Viola Moore, Nana Bryant.

1943

Silver Skates (Monogram) *D: Leslie Goodwins.* Kenny Baker, Patricia Morison, Belita, Frick and Frack, Irene Dare, Danny Shaw, Eugene Turner, Frank Faylen, Joyce Compton, Paul McVey, Ruth Lee, John Maxwell, Henry Wadsworth, George Stewart, JoAnn Dean, Ted Fio Rito and his Orchestra.

A Gentle Gangster (Republic) *D: Phil Rosen.* Barton MacLane, Molly Lamont, Dick Wessel, Jack LaRue, Joyce Compton, Cy Kendall, Rosella Towne, Ray Teal, Crane Whitley, Elliott Sullivan, Anthony Warde.

Let's Face It (Paramount) *D: Sidney Lanfield.* Bob Hope, Betty Hutton, ZaSu Pitts, Phyllis Povah, Dona Drake, Cully Richards, Eve Arden, Marjorie Weaver, Raymond Walburn, Joe Sawyer, Dave Willock, Andrew Tombes, Grace Hayle, Kay Linaker, Joyce Compton, Barbara Pepper, Robin Raymond, Phyllis Ruth, Emory Parnell, Eddie Dew, Eddie Dunn, Cyril Ring, William B. Davidson, Yvonne De Carlo, Noel Neill, Julie Gibson, Penny Edwards.

Joyce Compton and Al Pearce in Hitchhike to Happiness. COURTESY OF MATT HINRICHS.

Silver Spurs (Republic) *D: Joseph Kane.* Roy Rogers, Smiley Burnette, John Carradine, Phyllis Brooks, Joyce Compton, Jerome Cowan, Bob Nolan and the Sons of the Pioneers, Hal Taliaferro, Jack Kirk, Kermit Maynard, Dick Wessel, Forrest Taylor, Byron Foulger, Charles Wilson, Pat Brady, Jack O'Shea, Slim Whitaker, Arthur Loft, Eddy Waller, Tom London, Bud Osborne, Fred Burns, Henry Wills, "Trigger."

Swing Out the Blues (Columbia) *D: Malcolm St. Clair.* Bob Haymes, Lynn Merrick, Janis Carter, Tim Ryan, Joyce Compton, The Vagabonds, Arthur Q. Bryan, Kathleen Howard, John Eldredge, Dick Elliott, Lotte Stein, Tor Johnson.

1945

Pillow to Post (Warner Bros.) *D: Vincent Sherman.* Ida Lupino, Sydney Greenstreet, William Prince, Stuart Erwin, Ruth Donnelly, John Mitchell, Barbara Brown, Frank Orth, Regina Wallace, Willie Best, Paul Harvey, Carol Hughes, Bobby Blake, Anne O'Neil, Marie Blake, Victoria Horne, Lelah Tyler, Sue Moore, Don McGuire, Joyce Compton, Louis Armstrong and Orchestra, Grady Sutton.

Sydney Greenstreet, Reginald Gardiner, S.Z. Sakall, and Joyce in Christmas in Connecticut.

Hitchhike to Happiness (Republic) *D: Joseph Santley.* Al Pearce, Dale Evans, Brad Taylor (Stanley Brown), William Frawley, Jerome Cowan, Willy Trenk, Arlene Harris, Joyce Compton, Maude Eburne, Irving Bacon.

Christmas in Connecticut (Warner Bros.) *D: Peter Godfrey.* Barbara Stanwyck, Dennis Morgan, Sydney Greenstreet, Reginald Gardiner, S.Z. Sakall, Robert Shayne, Una O'Connor, Frank Jenks, Joyce Compton, Dick Elliott, Charles Arnt.

Mildred Pierce (Warner Bros.) *D: Michael Curtiz.* Joan Crawford, Zachary Scott, Jack Carson, Ann Blyth, Eve Arden, Bruce Bennett, George Tobias, Lee Patrick, Moroni Olson, JoAnn Marlowe, Barbara Brown, Charles Trowbridge, John Compton, Butterfly McQueen, Garry Owen, Clancy Cooper, Tom Dillon, James Flavin, Jack O'Connor, Charles Jordan, Robert Arthur, Joyce Compton, Lynne Baggett, Ramsay Ames, Leah Baird, John Christian, Joan Winfield, Chester Clute.

Danger Signal (Warner Bros.) *D: Robert Florey.* Faye Emerson, Zachary Scott, Richard Erdman, Rosemary De Camp, Bruce Bennett, Mona Freeman, Mary Servoss, Joyce Compton, Virginia Sale, Addison Richards, John Ridgely.

Roughly Speaking (Warner Bros.) *D: Michael Curtiz.* Rosalind Russell, Jack Carson, Robert Hutton, Jean Sullivan, Donald Woods, Craig Stevens, Ann Doran, Hobart Cavanaugh, Eily Malyon, Alan Hale, Jr., Robert Arthur, Ann Todd, Joyce Compton, Andy Clyde, Andrea King, Irving Bacon.

1946

Dark Alibi (Monogram) *D: Phil Karlson.* Sidney Toler, Benson Fong, Mantan Moreland, Teala Loring, George Holmes, Joyce Compton, John Eldredge, Russell Hicks, Tim Ryan, Janet Shaw, Edward Earle, Ray Walker, Milton Parsons, Edna Holland, Anthony Warde, George Eldridge.

Behind the Mask (Monogram) *D: Phil Karlson.* Kane Richmond, Barbara Read, George Chandler, Dorothea Kent, Joseph Crehan, Pierre Watkin, Robert Shayne, June Clyde, James Cardwell, Marjorie Hoshelle, Joyce Compton, Edward Gargan, Lou Crosby, Bill Christy, Nancy Brinkman, Dewey Robinson, Jean Carlin, Alura Stevens, Christine McIntyre, Marie Harmon, Ruth Cherrington.

Night and Day (Warner Bros.) *D: Michael Curtiz.* Cary Grant, Alexis Smith, Monty Woolley, Jane Wyman, Ginny Simms, Eve Arden, Victor Francen, Alan Hale, Dorothy Malone, Tom D'Andrea, Selena Royle, Donald Woods, Henry Stephenson, Paul Cavanagh, Sig Rumann, Clarence Muse, Herman Bing, Mary Martin, Joyce Compton,

Rendezvous with Annie (Republic) *D: Allan Dwan.* Eddie Albert, Faye Marlowe, Gail Patrick, Philip Reed, Sir C. Aubrey Smith, Raymond Walburn, William Frawley, James Mullican, Wallace Ford, George Chandler, Will Wright, Joyce Compton, Lucien Littlefield, Edwin Rand, Mary Field.

The Best Years of Our Lives (RKO-Goldwyn) *D: William Wyler.* Fredric March, Myrna Loy, Dana Andrews, Teresa Wright, Virginia Mayo, Cathy O'Donnel, Hoagy Carmichael, Harold Russell, Gladys George, Ray Collins, Steve Cochran, Minna Gombell, Joyce Compton.

1947

Scared to Death (Golden Gate) *D: Christy Cabanne.* Bela Lugosi, Nat Pendleton, George Zucco, Molly Lamont, Joyce Compton, Gladys Blake, Roland Varno, Douglas Fowley, Angelo Rossito, Lee Bennett.

Exposed (Republic) *D: George Blair.* Adele Mara, Robert E. Scott, Adrian Booth, Robert Armstrong, William Haade, Bob Steele, Harry Shannon, Charles Evans, Joyce Compton, Russell Hicks, Colin Campbell, Paul E. Burns, Edward Gargan, Mary Gordon, Patricia Knox.

Linda Be Good (Eagle-Lion) *D: Frank McDonald.* Elyse Knox, John Hubbard, Marie Wilson, Gordon Richards, Jack Norton, Ralph Sanford, Joyce Compton, Frank Scannell, Sir Lancelot, Professor Lamberti, The Cameo Girls.

1948

A Southern Yankee (MGM) *D: Edward Sedgwick.* Red Skelton, Brian Donlevy, Arlene Dahl, George Coulouris, Lloyd Gough, John Ireland, Minor Watson, Charles Dingle, Art Baker, Reed Hadley, Arthur Space, Joyce Compton.

Sorry, Wrong Number (Paramount) *D: Anatole Litvak.* Barbara Stanwyck, Burt Lancaster, Ann Richards, Wendell Corey, Harold Vermilyea, Ed Begley, Leif Erickson, William Conrad, John Bromfield, Jimmy Hunt, Dorothy Neumann, Paul Fierro, Kristine Miller, Suzanne Dalbert, George Stren, Joyce Compton, Tito Vuolo, Garry Owen, Holmes Herbert, Neal Dodd, Louise Lorimer, Yola D'Avril, Pepito Perez, Ashley Cowan, Cliff Clark.

1949

Incident (Monogram) *D: William Beaudine.* Warren Douglas, Jane Frazee, Robert Osterloh, Anthony Caruso, Joyce Compton, Harry Lauter, Eddie Dunn, Meyer Grace, Harry Cheshire, Lynn Millan, Robert Emmett Keane, Pierre Watkin, Ralph Dunn, John Shay.

Grand Canyon (Screen Guild) *D: Paul Landres.* Richard Arlen, Mary Beth Hughes, Reed Hadley, James Millican, Olin Howlin, Grady Sutton, Joyce Compton, Charlie Williams, Margie Dean, Anna May Slaughter, Stanley Price.

Mighty Joe Young (RKO) *D: Ernest B. Schoedsack.* Terry Moore, Ben Johnson, Robert Armstrong, Frank McHugh, Joseph Young, Douglas Fowley, Paul Guilfoyle, Nestor Paiva, Regis Toomey, James Flavin, Joyce Compton.

1950

Jet Pilot (Universal) *D: Josef von Sternberg.* John Wayne, Janet Leigh, Jay C. Flippen, Hans Conreid, Paul Fix, Richard Rober, Roland Winters, Ivan Triesault, John Bishop, Perdita Chandler, Joyce Compton, Denver Pyle.

The Persuader (Allied) *D: Dick Ross.* William Tallman, James Craig, Kristine Miller, Darryl Hickman, Georgia Lee, Alvy Moore, George Walcott, Joyce Compton,

1957

Girl in the Woods (Republic) *D: Tom Gries.* Forrest Tucker, Maggie Hayes, Barton MacLane, Diana Francis, Paul Langton, Murvyn Vye, Kim Charney, Mickey Finn, Diana Francis, Margaret Hayes, Joyce Compton.

PART V | The Eleanor Hunt Mystery

While Joyce became increasingly frustrated with writers who used "dumb blonde" to sum up her long career in films, she understood its origins and saw how the moniker could be perpetuated by writers who might not have seen her wide variety of film roles.

What she couldn't understand and what caused her frustration in her later years were the misunderstandings surrounding her name.

By her own admission and through independent research,[1] it is clear she was born Olivia Joyce Compton. She was quite perplexed that some writers erroneously associated her with other names.

Writers, she felt, used "their own imagination" to tell her story. "Some wrote that I'd changed my name to Dixie Belle Lee because of all my Southern roles and that my parents didn't like me being in films — ha! — when it was them who brought me to Hollywood to have a try. Now, I have another name to get rid of, the 'somebody' Hunt name."

How she became associated with Eleanor Hunt was a mystery to Joyce. However, most film references and some internet sites state emphatically that Eleanor Hunt is Joyce's birth name, insinuating that Joyce Compton is an adopted professional name — nonsense, of course!

Eleanor Hunt was a Ziegfeld girl who started her career on the New York stage. She was born Elinore Hunt to John and Katherine Hunt on January 10, 1910, in New York City.[2] A chorus girl in the New York stage production of *Whoopee!*, her role was elevated to Eddie Cantor's leading lady when some of the cast came to Hollywood to film the screen version in 1930.

Barbara Weeks, one of the chorus girls from *Whoopee!* who was brought West for the screen version and who went on to become a film actress in over 30 films during the 1930s, said she remembered the auburn-haired Hunt from their Ziegfeld days.

"Eleanor Hunt was a just a chorus girl in the New York version, but had the lead in the film version," Weeks remembered in 1996.[3] "There were lots of people interviewed for that part, but she got it, and I don't know how."

After the smashing success of *Whoopee!*, it looked as though Hunt's star was on the rise. She signed with Fox, yet her career in films never took off. She was leading lady to John Wayne in *Blue Steele* (1935) and played opposite silent film matinee idol Conrad Nagel in a number of films in the 1930s. Often her roles were little more than bits.

---

[1] The 1910 U.S. Census lists Olivia J. (Joyce), age three, living with her parents, H.W. and Golden M. Compton in Harrison, Oklahoma. Kentucky is listed as the state of her birth. The 1920 U.S. Census lists Joyce, age 12, living with her parents, Henry W. and Golden M. Compton, in Tulsa, Oklahoma.

[2] According to the 1920 U.S Census.

[3] Barbara Weeks interview with Michael G. Ankerich.

Married for a time to actor Rex Lease, Hunt retired from the screen in the early 1940s. She died in New York on June 12, 1981.

While Joyce and Eleanor Hunt were in the cast of *Good Sport* (1931), Joyce did not know or remember her from the film. It was only later that their names became intertwined. Joyce chalked it up to just one more mistake writers made in their efforts to document her life and career.

Eleanor Hunt and Paul Gregory in Whoopee!

INDEX

Adventures of Jim Bowie, The (TV) 236
Affairs of a Gentleman (1934) 148, 263
Afraid to Talk (1932) 262
Allan, Hugh 17
Allwyn, Astrid 149
Ankles Preferred (1927) 256
Annabelle's Affairs (1931) 259
Arden, Eve 188
Artists and Models Abroad (1938) 27, 178, 272
Arzner, Dorothy 96
Astor, Mary 19, 21, 80, 182, 183, 267, 275
Awful Truth, The (1937) 29, 174-175, 178, 270
Ayres, Lew 271

Baggot, Lynn 188
Balalaika (1939) 274
Barrymore, John 126
Beauty Parlor (1932), 27, 260
Bedtime Story (1941) 278
Beery, Wallace 126
Behind the Mask (1946) 281
Bell, Rex 98, 112
Bellamy, Madge 96, 162
Bennett, Constance 120
Benny, Jack 178
Bern, Paul 23, 118
Best Years of Our Lives, The (1946) 192, 281
Big Fibber, The (short) (1933) 263
Blackmon, Avis 192-195
Blue Steele (1935) 286
Blues in the Night (1941) 277
Blythe, Betty 150
Bogart, Humphrey 120
Bond, Ward 103
Border Cavalier, The (1927) 28, 192, 256
Born Reckless (1937) 269

Bow, Clara 21-22, 96-98, 112
Bradley, H.C. 260
Brent, Evelyn 74, 84
Brian, Mary 21, 80
Broadway Lady (1925) 256
Brooks, Phyllis 164
Brown, Johnny Mack 28, 162-163

Caliente Love (1933) 28, 262
Cantor, Eddie 286
Carroll, John 192
Carroll, Lucia 188
Catlett, Walter 146
Chandler, Helen 103, 104, 259
Chase, Charley 27, 28, 147
China Passage (1937) 269
Christmas in Connecticut (1945) 30, 280
Churchill, Marguerite 104
City for Conquest (1940) 275
Clark, Bobby 28
Classic Images 12
Clive, C.C. 266
Cody, Lew 150
College Scandal (1935) 265
Collier, Ruth 146
Collyer, June 110
Compton, Joyce; ambitions of 64-67, 126-127; appearance of 64, 75, 188, 252; artistic talent of 92-93, 248-249, 250; beauty contest 70-72; birth of 14, 46; breaks into talkies 21, 96-98; builds house in Sherman Oaks 158-159; buys property in Sherman Oaks 154; comedic style of 21, 27, 33, 146, 149-150; confusion of Eleanor Hunt as real name of 14, 286-287; death of 33; death of father 31, 242-245; death of grandmother

54; death of mother 30, 210-211; dumb
blonde image of 12, 27; early childhood
46-61; fashions and JC 72, 80, 108, 119,
120, 122, 179; financial situation of 32, 49,
73, 75, 92, 126-127, 248; First National
contract 75; first trip to California 64-67;
Fox contract of 23, 85, 108; Fox makeover
23; health of 31-33, 103, 192, 248; home
in Beverly Glen 116-122; home on
Edenhurst Avenue 92, 130; home on N.
Hobart Avenue 70; honored with star on
Hollywood Boulevard 31, 148; loses First
National contract 21,89; loses Fox contract
25, 127, 130; loses life savings 25, 126-127;
love of animals 93; marriage to William
(Bill) Kahiler 31, 224-232, 236; named a
Wampas Baby Star 19, 20, 80, 81, 182-184;
nursing work of 30-31, 236-237, 248;
opinions of self 33, 168, 253; relationship
with "Darrell" 88-89; relationship with
"Steve" 206-207; relationship with "Walter"
196-198; relationship with Abby Dreyfess
140-142, 154-155; relationship with Avis
Blackmon 192-195; relationship with
fans 13, 120, 251; relationship with gay
minister 218-220; relationship with George
O'Brien 23; relationship with Hugh Allan
17; relationship with Joel McCrea 25,
112-113; relationship with William Wyler
192; religious faith of 127, 202-203, 250;
reluctance of JC to date fellows actors 23,
104; screen test of 15; shyness of 72,76; start
of Hollywood career 15, 70; studio politics
and JC 19, 84-85, 151; support of family
13, 214-215, 236-237; trip to New York 27,
136-142; turns down Paramount contract
22; western films and JC 28, 96, 163-164;
writing of memoirs 38-40
Cooper, Gary 147, 148, 261
Costello, Dolores 21, 80
Country Gentlemen (1936) 169, 268
Courtney, Inez 182
Crawford, Joan 19, 21, 80

Daddy Knows Best (short) (1933) 28, 146, 263
Danger Signal (1945) 280
Dangerous Curves (1929) 21, 22, 96, 103, 257
Dark Alibi (1946) 281
Davis, Bette 252

Day, Marceline 21, 80
De Kerekjarto, Duci 169
De Mille, Cecil B. 15, 73
Dee, Francis 113
Del Rio, Dolores 19, 21, 80
Dietrich, Marlene 84, 188, 192
Dream Stuff (1933) 28, 263
Dresser, Louise 110, 122
Dunne, Irene 29, 174

Eilers, Francis 203
Eilers, Leonard 203
Ellis Island (1936) 268
Escape to Paradise (1939) 274
Evans, Dr. Louis 203
Everything's Ducky (1934) 28, 263
Exposed (1947) 282

False Faces (1932) 261
Farrell, Charles 23, 110, 111
Faye, Alice 84, 273
Fazenda, Louise 110
Fighting for Justice (1932) 28, 163, 261
Fleming, Rhonda 203
Flying Irishman, The (1939) 274
Ford, John 23, 103, 104
French, Charles K. 162

Gable, Clark 192
Gardner, Jack 122
Gargan, William 182
Gaynor, Janet 19, 21, 23, 80, 85, 110
Gentle Gangster, A (1943) 278
Girl in the Woods (1957) 236, 283
Gish, Lillian 64
Gittleson, June 149
Go Into Your Dance (1935) 264
Going Places (1938) 272
Golden Bed, The (1925) 17, 73, 256
Good Sport (1931) 259, 287
Graham, Rev. Billy 203
Grand Canyon (1949) 282
Grant, Cary 29, 174-175, 192
Gregory, Paul 287
Griffith, Corinne 19, 74, 84
Guard, Alisa 31

Haines, Connie 203
Hallam Cooley Agency 146

Harlow, Jean 23, 118
Harvester, The (1936) 268
Hat Check Girl (1932) 261
High Society Blues (1930) 110, 257
Hillman, Eddie 169, 171
Hitchhike to Happiness (1945) 280
Hollywood Christian Group 201-203
Hollywood Hobbies (short) (1935) 267
Honeymoon Deferred (1940) 274
Hopper, Hedda 110
Hotel for Women (1939) 274
How to Watch Football (short) (1938) 272
Hubbard, John 182
Hughes, Howard 136-137
Hume, Fred 28
Hunt, Eleanor 14, 286-287
Hussey, Ruth 271
Hyams, Leila 148

I Take This Oath (1940) 275
I Take This Woman (1940) 277
If I had a Million (1932) 147-148, 248, 262
Imitation of Life (1934) 264
Incident (1949) 282

Janney, William 103
Jason, Al 273
Jet Pilot (1950) 283
Johnson, Chic 169
Johnson, Joe 136

Kahiler, William "Bill" F. 31, 224-232, 236
Karns, Roscoe 148
Kibbee, Guy 245
Kid Galahad (1937) 27, 269
King Kelly of the U.S.A. (1934) 263
Kingston, Al 146
Kirkland, Muriel 149
Knockout Kisses (1933) 28, 263

La Rocque, Rod 15, 73
Lady and Gent (1932) 260
Landis, Carole 182, 183, 275
Langdon, Harry 126
Last Warning, The (1939) 273
Lear, Bill 169
Lear, Moya 169
Lease, Rex 287

Lebedeff, Ivan 148, 149
Lee, Lila 148, 150
Leisen, Mitchell "Mitch" 178-179
Lena Rivers (1932) 260
Let 'Em Have It (1935) 265
Let's Face It (1943) 278
Let's Make Music (1940) 276
Liebman, Roy 19
Life Hesitates at 40 (short) (1935) 28, 266
Lightnin' (1930) 25, 111-112, 257
Linda Be Good (1948) 282
Littlefield, Lucien 147
Livingstone, Mary 179
Lloyd, Harold 119
Long, Sally 21, 80
Love Before Breakfast (1936) 267
Love on a Budget (1938) 272
Lukas, Paul 148

Madison Sq. Garden (1932) 262
Magnificent Obsession (1935) 27, 265
Maltin, Leonard 33
Manhattan Monkey Business (1935) 27, 28, 147, 266
Manpower (1940) 149, 188-189, 277
Man-Proof (1938) 272
March, Fredric 22
Marion, Edna 21, 80
Marlowe, Don 248
Marsh, Joan 258
Mason, Shirley 17
Mathis, June 75
Max Factor 73
McCoy, Tim 163
McCrea, Joel 25, 104, 111-113
McCullough, Paul 28
McPhail, Addie 110
Menjou, Adolphe 182
Mercer, Beryl 148
Merkel, Una 85
Mighty Joe Young (1949) 282
Mildred Pierce (1945) 27, 30, 280
Million Dollar Ransom (1934) 263
Moon Over Her Shoulder (1941) 277
Moore, Colleen 74, 75, 84
Morriss, Ann 271
Mr. Dynamite (1935) 265
Murder with Pictures (1936) 268
Murray, Mae 15-16, 64, 70, 74, 75

Nagel, Conrad 286
Night and Day (1946) 281
Nilsson, Anna Q. 74, 84
Not Exactly Gentlemen (1931) 258

O'Brien, George 23, 103, 104
O'Neil, Sally 21, 80
O'Sullivan, Maureen 29, 178, 271
Oakie, Jack 126, 147, 148, 248
Oakie, Victoria Horne 248
Oakman, Wheeler 260
Olsen, Ole 169
Only Yesterday (1933) 262
Orr, Dr. Irwin 202

Parisian Romance, A (1932) 261
Parsons, Louella 120
Patrick, John 17
Pearce, Al 279
Pendleton, Nat 267
Persuader, The (1950) 283
Pete and Gladys (TV) 236, 242
Pick a Star (1937) 269
Pickford, Mary 64
Pidgeon, Walter 28, 29, 179
Pillow to Post (1945) 279
Plumber and the Lady, The (short) (1933) 28, 263
Public Ghost No. 1 (short) (1935) 28, 266

Raft, George 149, 151, 189
Rendezvous with Annie (1946) 281
Reno (1939) 274
Revier, Dorothy 260
Reynolds, Vera 21, 80
Rhythm in the Clouds (1937) 269
Rich, Lillian 73
Richard Diamond, Private Detective (TV) 236
Roach, Hal 175, 183-184
Roach, Margaret 183
Roadhouse Queen (short) (1933) 28, 263
Robards, Jason 148
Rocket, Al 75
Rogers, Dale Evans 203, 248
Rogers, Roy 164, 203, 248
Rogers, Will 25, 111, 112
Rose of Washington Square (1939) 273
Roughly Speaking (1945) 281
Royer (fashion designer) 275

Russell, Jane 203
Rustlers of Red Dog (1935) 28, 162-163, 169, 264

Sally (1925) 256
Scared to Death (1947) 281
Scattergood Meets Broadway (1941) 277
Schlank, Bess 80
School for Girls (1935) 266
Scott, Randolph 174
Sea Racketeers (1937) 270
Sennett, Mack 28, 146
7th Heaven (1927) 23
She Asked for It (1937) 270
Sheehan, Howard 122, 126
Sheehan, Winfield "Winnie" 85, 110, 119, 120
Silver Skates (1943) 278
Silver Spurs (1943) 28, 164, 279
Sing, Sinners, Sing (1933) 148, 262
Sitting on the Moon (1936) 268
Skelton, Red 193
Sky Hawk, The (1930) 257
Sky Murder (1940) 28, 179, 276
Small Town Boy (1937) 270
Soft Living (1928) 162, 256
Sorry, Wrong Number (1948) 30, 282
Southern Yankee, A (1948) 30, 193, 282
Spencer, Tim 203
Spider, The (1931) 258
Spring Madness (1937) 29, 178, 272
Spurr, Melbourne 149
Star for a Night (1936) 27, 268
Street Angel (1928) 23
Suicide Squad (1935) 266
Sunny Side Up (1929) 23
Swanson, Gloria 120
Swing Out the Blues (1943) 279
Syncopating Sue (1926) 19, 256
Salute (1929) 22, 23, 103, 104, 108, 257

Talbot, Lyle 148, 267
Tashman, Lilyan 150
Taylor, Elizabeth 192
Teasdale, Verree 182
They Drive By Night (1940) 149, 275
Three Girls Lost (1931) 258
Three Sisters, The (1930) 110, 257
Three Smart Girls (1936) 267
Thunder Birds (1942) 278

Toast of New York, The (1937) 27, 248, 269
Too Many Women (1942) 278
Top of the Town (1937) 269
Townsend, Colleen 202
Trade Winds (1938) 272
Trapped by Television (1936) 268
Trumpet Blows, The (1934) 149, 263
Turnabout (1940) 30, 182-184, 188, 274
Under 18 (1932) 259
Under Your Spell (1936) 26
Unholy Love (1932) 148, 260
Up Pops the Devil (1931) 258

Valentino, Rudolph 15, 23, 70, 119
Valley of the Lawless (1936) 28, 163, 267
Villain Still Pursued Her, The (1940) 276

Walsh, Raoul 188
Wampas (Western Association of Motion
  Picture Advertisers) 19, 21, 80, 81
Wampas Baby Stars: A Biographical Dictionary
  (book) 19
Warner, H.B. 148, 150
Wayne, John 103, 286

We Have Our Moments (1937) 271
Weeks, Barbara 286
Wells, Jacqueline 271
Westward Passage (1932) 260
What Fools Men (1925) 17, 256
White Parade, The (1934) 29, 149, 150, 264
Who Killed Aunt Maggie? (1940) 276
Whoopee! (1930) 286, 287
Wild Company (1930) 257
Wild Party, The (1929) 21, 22, 96, 257
Wilson, Dorothy 150
Wilson, Lois 150
Wind, The (1928) 46
Wings Over Honolulu (1937) 271
Women Are Like That (1938) 271
Women of All Nations (1931) 259
Wray, Fay 19, 21, 80
Wrestlers, The (short) (1933) 262
Wyler, William 192

You and Me (1938) 149, 272
Young, Loretta 29, 149, 258

Ziegfeld Girl (1941) 277

ABOUT THE AUTHOR

Michael G. Ankerich is the author of *Broken Silence: Conversations with 23 Silent Film Stars* and *The Sound of Silence: Conversations with 16 Film and Stage Personalities Who Bridged the Gap Between Silents and Talkies.* He has written extensively for *Classic Images* and *Films of the Golden Age*.

He is currently working on *Dangerous Curves atop Hollywood Heels: The Careers, Lives, and Misfortunes of 22 Hard Luck Girls of the Silent Screen*, which will feature the stories of Olive Borden, Lucille Ricksen, Eve Southern, Barbara La Marr, Wanda Hawley, Alberta Vaughn, Elinor Fair, Dorothy Sebastian, and others.

A former newspaper reporter, he is a technical writer, and lives with his partner, Charlie, and their two girls, MaeBelle and Ms. Taylor, in Georgia.

Breinigsville, PA USA
14 August 2010
243591BV00004B/70/P